The BEGINNING RUNNER'S JOURNAL

DR. LAURA G. FARRES & THE SPORT MEDICINE COUNCIL
OF BRITISH COLUMBIA

with LYNDA CANNELL & DREW MITCHELL

The BEGINNING
RUNNER'S
JOURNAL

GREYSTONE BOOKS

Douglas & McIntyre Publishing Group
Vancouver/Toronto/New York

SportMedBC, with principal contributors Lynda Cannell (Executive Director) and Drew Mitchell (Manager of Sport Health Programs), is a not for profit society and network of sport medicine and science professionals practising in British Columbia. The organization's mission is to identify, develop and promote best practices in sport health, sport safety and sport training.

03 04 05 06 07   5 4 3 2 1

Greystone Books
A division of Douglas & McIntyre Ltd.
2323 Quebec Street, Suite 201
Vancouver, British Columbia
Canada v5T 4s7

National Library of Canada Cataloguing in Publication Data
Farres, Laura G. (Laura Gillian), 1966–
    The beginner runner's journal / Laura G. Farres, and the Sport Medicine Council
    of British Columbia.

    ISBN 1-55054-965-0

    1. Running. 2. Diaries (Blank-books) I. Sport Medicine Council of B.C. II. Title.
GV1061.F37 2003   613.7'172   C2002-911238-9

Editing by Barbara Tomlin
Cover and interior design by Peter Cocking
Cover photograph by Stuart McCall/North Light Images
Printed and bound in Canada by Transcontinental
Distributed in the U.S. by Publishers Group West

The publisher gratefully acknowledges the support of the Canada Council for the Arts and of the British Columbia Arts Council. The publisher also acknowledges the financial support of the Government of Canada through the Book Publishing Industry Development Program (BPIDP) for its publishing activities.

CONTENTS

It is good to have an end to

journey toward, but it is the

journey that matters, in the end.

URSULA K. LE GUIN

INTRODUCTION

Welcome to *The Beginning Runner's Journal.* This book is for anyone who wants to start a walk/run program. Perhaps you used to be active and you want to become active again. Perhaps you want to lose a little weight. Maybe you want to become fitter. Or maybe you want to train for a specific race or event. Whatever your reason for starting a walk/run program, *The Beginning Runner's Journal* can help you achieve your goals.

This book provides you with training support based on the popular 13-week walk/run program featured in *The Beginning Runner's Handbook* (Greystone, 2001). At the heart of *The Beginning Runner's Journal* are pages for daily journal entries. You can use these pages to record your thoughts and feelings and your progress. In addition, this book contains specific goal-setting and motivational exercises. These exercises and the many opportunities for reflection they provide will help you move beyond the scope of other training diaries that ask you to merely set a few goals and record your mileage, pace and distance.

The Beginning Runner's Journal is designed to help you:

- Set your own standards and measures of improvement
- Make appropriate choices to facilitate your personal growth in the area of fitness
- Push yourself beyond the boundaries of your past experiences
- Try new things to achieve the results you want

Making fitness a regular part of your life takes a strong commitment, a desire to improve and a willingness to make changes. Using the exercises and journal pages in this book can help you maintain your commitment, find new ways to improve and cope with change.

Why you should keep a training journal

Keeping a journal can help you set challenging and realistic goals, assess the effects of your training, monitor your progress, stay motivated, avoid over-training and injury, and enjoy your training more. Perhaps the greatest benefit of keeping a journal is the opportunity it provides to consistently monitor your thoughts, feelings and actions, and to make you more aware of the impact of these elements on your behaviours. This awareness allows you to identify your strengths, analyse challenges and make positive adjustments along the way.

If you are like most people who begin a walk/run program, you will need to make some changes in your life and daily routine in order to accommodate and stick with training. If you are resistant to these changes, make too many changes at once, set unrealistic goals or expect immediate success, then staying motivated and sticking with your program will be difficult. Be patient and approach your training in a realistic manner. Change is a process and this book can facilitate that process.

What you need to know about change

Making lifestyle changes isn't easy, but understanding four things about change can help.

1. Change can be gradual. Beginning a walk/run program will likely entail making a number of changes to your present lifestyle, including your daily priorities and your diet. Don't be intimidated by this process, as changes do not have to occur all at once. Indeed, training programs that try to change too much too fast are doomed to fail. Too much change at once can make you lose confidence in your ability to achieve your goals. In the simplest terms, all you need to do at the beginning is find about one hour for training, three times a week. You can add other elements as you go along if you want to make the program more challenging or complex. But initially, if you are concerned about the amount of change that has to occur, then choose a road that is a little easier and build your confidence.

2. Change involves several stages. Change occurs in stages (six of them, in fact) and you will often move back and forth through these stages until you finally reach a point where training is part of your regular routine. In essence, you will progress from not thinking you need or want to do a walk/run program to automatically making daily choices based on the program goals. There are certain strategies to help you negotiate each stage, and knowing the stage you are in can help you learn how to move through it more effectively. (See Chapter 1 for more detail.)

3. Preparing and planning for change helps. Personal routines or plans should be based on your individual needs. These plans can help you stick with the program and overcome any obstacles or setbacks you might face. Most people have days filled with countless routines. Since it is easier to stick with the routines and habits you know, you are going to have to work at changing some of these in order to achieve your walk/run goals.

For instance, it is much easier to come home from work and turn on the TV than it is to put on your gear and go outside for your workout (especially on those cold rainy days). Taking a new path and feeling better about your resulting actions is difficult at first but more rewarding in the end. As the poet Robert Frost suggests in "The Road Not Taken,"

> *Two roads diverged in a wood, and I—*
> *I took the one less traveled by,*
> *And that has made all the difference.*

4. Setbacks are part of the process. Training does not always go according to plan: injuries occur, motivation wanes, personal issues arise and work and family commitments intervene. Making the choices that are good for you takes work and, ultimately, becomes a journey of self-discovery. Your path to change should be viewed as an ongoing learning process. Personal setbacks and challenges should be taken as a natural and meaningful part of the process. Be patient with yourself as you move along the road. Bumps and small detours are a natural part of your journey and no change is perfect or occurs immediately. It is the journey, not the destination that will truly be your biggest accomplishment.

How you can use this journal

The Beginning Runner's Journal consists of four chapters that prepare you for training, pages to write about your training experience and appendixes that describe two different training programs.

Chapter 1 will help you develop a personal motivation plan. Exercises and questions give you an opportunity to reflect, gain knowledge about yourself and stay motivated on a day-to-day basis.

Chapter 2 provides technical information associated with successful, injury-free walking/running. There is advice about managing your health, body and mind, and specific tips that you may choose to incorporate into your weekly training plans.

Chapter 3 will help you make a commitment to your plan. Exercises challenge you to identify your priorities, determine your program schedule, set your goals and make a plan for the road ahead.

Chapter 4 explains how to use the journal pages.

The journal pages provide space for 26 weeks of daily entries. The pages are divided into two 13-week blocks. This means that you can follow the introductory walk/run program described in Appendix A and then continue, if you choose, with the walk/run maintenance program described in Appendix B. (This allows for six months of training—the time needed to make changes stick.) There is space to record your thoughts and feelings, rate the intensity of your workout and rate how you felt mentally and physically. At the end of each week and at a six-week mid point, there is space to write about your highlights and make adjustments to your goals and personal motivation plan. At the end of the first 13-week block, a series of exercises will help you celebrate your accomplishments, identify hurdles, make modifications to your personal motivation plan and move forward into the second 13-week training block. The journal pages conclude with some exercises to help you review your overall experience, identify the lessons learned and move on as a dedicated walker or runner.

Appendix A includes the 13-week walk/run program described in *The Beginning Runner's Handbook*. **Appendix B** describes a 13-week walk/run maintenance program.

The Beginning Runner's Journal will guide you through both the 13-week walk/run program and the 13-week walk/run maintenance program and make walking or running a regular part of your life. All you need to do is find the time and follow the schedule. Enjoy the process!

If we wait for the moment when

everything, absolutely everything is

ready, we shall never begin.

IVAN TURGENEV

FIRST STEPS

There is more to starting a walk/run program than just heading out the door. Because you are trying to make changes that you hope will become lifelong habits, you will need to lay a strong foundation for these changes. You can use this chapter to develop a foundation—your own personal motivation plan. This plan will address your individual needs and help you start and stick with a fitness regimen.

Getting ready for change

Changing your actions or incorporating new behaviours such as running or walking into your life can be challenging. There are six stages that most people move through as they try to make regular physical activity part of their daily routine. See if you can identify with one of these specific stages.

Stage 1: "I wasn't even thinking of starting a walk/run program—someone gave me this book." This is the *pre-contemplative* stage. You are not thinking about or planning to make the program part of your life any time soon. If you picked up this book, then you are probably beyond this stage. However, if someone gave you this book you might be in this stage. It is not that you don't want to change; you just may not be aware of how you can benefit from the program. You probably need a little convincing that all this walk/run stuff is worthwhile.

Stage 2: "It sounds like a good idea, but . . ." This is the *contemplative* stage. Now you are beginning to think about starting the program some time in the future. In this stage, you are aware that a walk/run program is a good idea and that incorporating it into your life would probably be beneficial. However, you are not sure if you are ready or if the time is right. There always seem to be reasons *not* to start. If this sounds like you, you will need to challenge your "buts" and talk back to your excuses. You will need to seize the moment and get ready to make the commitment.

Stage 3: "Tell me more. I am ready to make the commitment." This is the *preparation* stage. You are planning to make the program part of your life in the very near future. You may be seeking information about the training and its requirements. At this point, you can best help yourself by clearly outlining your commitment, setting your goals and making a plan to achieve these goals. You will need to be wary of getting stuck in this phase (remember that exercise equipment collecting dust in your closet?).

Stage 4: "I am doing it." This is the *action* stage. You are physically active and have been for the past few weeks or months. You are acting on your goals and carrying out your plans. This stage requires the most commitment and energy. The key here is to continue to celebrate your training accomplishments and reward yourself for each small success along the way. The road is long and after a little while your motivation may wane or your family and friends may stop recognizing your accomplishments. Having a personal motivation plan can help here. At this point your actions are more important than ever because you want training to become part of your routine and to be rewarding in its own right.

Stage 5: "I love it and can't imagine my life without it." This is the *maintenance* stage. You are regularly active now and have been for more than six months. You are enjoying the process and view your training as an integrated and important part of your life. You have developed solid routines, associations and expectations that will allow you to keep running or walking. Great job! The key is to keep challenging yourself and to find new and interesting ways to keep your motivation up and your interest piqued. Setting new goals is important here.

Stage 6: "Oops." This is the *relapse* stage. The reality is that most people do not follow a straight path to the "I love it" stage (and even the "I love it" people experience an "oops" sometimes). Somewhere along the way you may experience setbacks or meet obstacles that prevent you from sticking with training. All of a sudden, you may find yourself at an earlier stage of change. You may feel discouraged or see yourself as a failure. This may be the point where you have dropped out or stopped other programs. *Don't give up.* You are learning a skill. Don't expect immediate success. The reality is that most people revisit the stages at some point, but the strategies for moving through them remain the same. It is important not to become overwhelmed by the setback. You simply need to view your setbacks as minor stumbles in the road, not as outright falls. You can find your footing and once again enjoy the beautiful road ahead.

Do any of these stages sound familiar? Can you identify the stage you are in right now? Once you know your stage, you are ready to develop your personal motivation plan.

Understanding your reasons for training

It is important to identify your reasons for beginning a walk/run program. These reasons are your long-term goals. Some people begin a walk/run program to become healthier and fitter, others to improve their appearance and still others start training to challenge themselves. When you identify your reasons you should also try to define specific end points that are meaningful for you. These indicators will tell you when you have accomplished what you set out to do. For example, you may feel satisfied when you have lost a certain amount of weight or you can run 10 km or you are regularly active at least three times a week. Knowing your reasons and your end points can help guide your thoughts, feelings and actions, and allow you to see your progress.

Jot down as many reasons as you can think of in the space provided and describe your end points.

Exercise: Reasons to walk/run

What are my reasons for doing a walk/run program?

_____

_____

_____

How will I know when I have achieved what I set out to do?

_____

_____

Take a moment now and examine your reasons for starting a walk/run program. How do they make you feel? If you are a little anxious, don't worry. Your reasons may seem rather daunting until you break them down into more manageable goals. You will be able to do that later in this book. Also, remember that it is reasonable at this stage to be questioning whether you have the ability and skills necessary to carry out the program. You will be able to explore that later too.

If you had trouble identifying your reasons to start a walk/run program, then you might consider weighing the pros and cons of starting. Use the exercise below to identify the advantages and the disadvantages of starting or not starting the program for you and for those people close to you. Check off the advantages and disadvantages you agree with and list any others you can think of.

Exercise: Starting a walk/run program

Advantages

☐ I would feel better about myself.

☐ I would have more energy for my _____
(hobbies, job, family…).

☐ I would feel less stressed.

_____

_____

_____

Disadvantages

☐ I would get out of breath when I run and I hate that feeling.

☐ I'm too tired at the end of the day.

☐ It's boring.

_____

_____

_____

Not starting a walk/run program

Advantages

☐ I would have more time to _____
(read, garden, clean the house...).

_____

_____

_____

Disadvantages

☐ I would still be out of shape.
☐ I would still be frustrated with my inactivity.

_____

_____

_____

Are there enough reasons to make a walk/run program part of your life? If so, your next step is to develop a strong vision of your journey towards becoming a walker or runner.

Your personal vision

Runners and walkers come in different shapes, sizes and ability levels. Regardless of the differences, as soon as these people leave home to work out, they are all striving towards their own fitness visions. Having a vision of yourself as a fit and athletic person gives you an important goal to work towards.

So what is your walk/run vision? You may never have thought of yourself as athletic or fit, so it means challenging your past images and redefining what being athletic or fit means to you. The object is to have your own definition of what you would like for yourself and then imagine what would be possible if you were able to achieve the vision.

Begin by doing this imagery exercise. You can have someone read the script to you, or you can read the script first and then close your eyes and take yourself through it.

Exercise: Imagery script

Imagine yourself one year into the future. You have been doing a walk/run consistently for the past year.

Take a deep breath and see, hear and feel the image of yourself as clearly and as vividly as you can. Pay close attention to every detail about yourself: what you look like (pause 10 seconds), where you are (pause 10 seconds), what you are wearing (pause 10 seconds) and who is around you (pause 10 seconds). Notice how you move and hold yourself (pause 10 seconds).

- What stands out for you about this new self? (pause 10 seconds)
- What surprises you about this self? (pause 10 seconds)
- What inspires you about this self? (pause 10 seconds)
- Now open your eyes and complete the following:

1. Write down your vision of yourself in as much detail as possible.

---

2. What stood out for you about this new self?

_____

_____

3. What surprised you about this self?

_____

_____

4. What inspired you about this self?

_____

_____

5. How does the image of yourself in the future fit with the image of yourself right now?

_____

_____

6. What changes would you need to make to move towards your vision?

_____

_____

_____

7. What are the biggest obstacles to achieving your vision?

_____

_____

If you have trouble coming up with a vision for yourself, don't despair. Sometimes it takes a little work to develop a vision. Another way to do this is to use other people as models. There are many people out there who have changed their lives and achieved their fitness visions. These people are not elite athletes—just runners and walkers who have made fitness part of their lives. You can read about them in the newspaper, or you can see them at the finish line of any walk/run event. It is easy to recognize them because they have big smiles on their faces as they cross the finish line, they have their family and friends cheering their accomplishment and, more importantly, they look just like you.

Think of people like you who have achieved what you would like to achieve.

People who help me believe that I can:
Alicia Snell of Oakville, Ontario. In late 1998, Snell weighed 150 kg (328 pounds), wheezed when she walked and couldn't have run for a single kilometre. She started a training program that included weights and running. On April 14, 2002, at 46 years of age and 70 kg (155 pounds) she completed the Boston Marathon. Today, when friends ask Snell for her "secret," she says, "There is no magic elixir, only commitment. What you eat and your exercise routine must be your first priority. And one without the other doesn't work. That is tough in today's ultra-busy world, but I don't see any other way that's going to last a lifetime."

Having a walk/run vision allows you to explore possibilities and strive to achieve your potential. A vision gives you a sense of purpose and provides you with information about yourself. Seeing yourself as a successful walker/runner is the first step to believing that it can happen. With that belief, you can challenge obstacles that may be preventing you from achieving what you would like.

Summarize the qualities of the person you would like to be in the space provided. Revisit this vision statement as often as you can for inspiration, direction and motivation.

My vision statement:

_____

_____

_____

_____

_____

_____

_____

Your personal mission statement

Defining who you are can be another powerful way to help you make the changes you desire. A personal mission statement is like a credo or motto that states what your life is about. It should reflect the values you hold about the importance of health and fitness and life in general. It can act as a guide to help you adhere to what you truly want to achieve. It can help you commit to a fitness program.

A personal mission statement can be anything you want—a favourite quotation, song lyrics or your own creation. It needs to inspire you and help you remember what you are all about. Here are two examples of mission statements:

- Each week I thank the people who support my dream.
- Each day I get out the door I celebrate my accomplishments.
- Each step I take I recognize it as one more step towards my vision.
- Each moment I realize that I can be as strong as I need or want to be.

B Be everything I know I can be in all areas of my life.

E Encourage my strengths along with my weaknesses.

C Challenge myself to train smart and to live well.

O Organize my time—the most valuable thing I have to share.

M Move it. Nothing has ever changed when I stood still.

E Expect nothing less than the best I can give every day.

To develop your own mission statement, begin by thinking about the following questions.

- What are my greatest strengths?
- What strengths do others see in me?
- What things are important to me?
- What qualities do I most admire in others?
- What am I not doing in my life that I would like to be doing?
- What am I doing that I am happy with?
- What activities do I consider of greatest value?
- What important principles guide my actions?
- How would I like to live my life?

After you have thought about these questions and about your values and your vision of yourself as a fit and healthy person, write your mission statement in the space provided. Post this mission statement on your wall and review it regularly.

My mission statement:

_____

_____

_____

_____

_____

_____

_____

Overcoming obstacles

Identifying the obstacles that stand in the way of change is an important part of the process. Often these obstacles or hurdles to training take the form of excuses. These excuses may be based on fears that you can learn to overcome.

Some people fear making changes in general, others fear looking silly when they start to work out. Still others fear that their bodies might change or they might be injured. Excuses protect you from risk and failure, redirect your focus and limit your opportunities for success. The key is to understand your excuses and explore ways to challenge and resolve them.

Consider the examples in the chart below. Check off any that apply to you and then add other personal hurdles you can think of and your ideas for handling them.

Exercise: Handling hurdles

Personal hurdles to achieving my fitness goals	How can I overcome this hurdle?
Lack of time ☐ I have too many things on the go and there is no way I can find time to work out.	☐ I could be better with my time. I could try to squeeze in a workout at lunch or when I take my kids to soccer practice.
My children ☐ When I come home from work, I want to spend time with my kids.	☐ I could take them with me. Maybe they could ride their bikes or roller-blade.
An injury ☐ My knees hurt a lot when I start to walk or run.	☐ I could see my doctor or physiotherapist to learn if there is anything I can do to make my knees stronger.

Building confidence

Not believing in yourself can stop you from achieving your goals. If you are feeling less than confident in your ability to engage in a walk/run program now, you need to understand how belief and your behaviour are linked. If you do not believe you can accomplish something, then you probably will not. Belief affects your thoughts, feelings, image of yourself and, ultimately, your actions. Psychologist Albert Bandura coined the term "self-efficacy" and defined it as an individual's belief in his or her ability to accomplish a particular objective. Starting a walk/run program, staying with it, challenging yourself to improve, dealing with your successes and setbacks—all of these take belief. There are a number of factors that influence your belief system and a number of strategies that you can use to help build your belief in your ability to achieve your fitness goals.

Identify your personal successes

Previous successful experiences in your life can help you see that you have the capacity to succeed and stick with a walk/run program. You possess all the necessary skills to achieve the success you desire. Every day you balance the various components of your life: you manage your time, you make and keep appointments, you follow routines, you overcome obstacles and you successfully deal with stress and anxiety in order to complete a task. However, you may not recognize or celebrate these abilities.

Use the exercise on the next page to learn more about what has contributed to your successes.

Exercise: Analysing personal successes

Note times in your life when you have succeeded. What qualities, skills and abilities contributed to your success in these instances?

Performed well

_____

Received praise for something I did

_____

Overcame obstacles

_____

Extended my limits to achieve

_____

Learned and mastered something new

_____

Balanced a number of projects

_____

Turn your abilities into affirmations

Once you have identified some of your qualities, skills and abilities, think about expressing each one as an affirmation. These strongly worded positive statements can be powerful reminders of the abilities you possess.

Exercise: Writing affirmations

SKILL/QUALITY/ABILITY	AFFIRMATION
Organized	I am an organized person.
Perseverant	I am persistent in pursuit of my goals.
Able to deal with pressure effectively	I perform well under pressure.

Think about writing other more general affirmations as well. For example:

- I believe in myself and my potential.
- I can achieve anything I set out to do.
- I am completely in control of my choices and my life.
- I can learn new things and make the changes I want.
- I am a fit and healthy person.

Affirmations that are meaningful to you can be used on a daily basis to push out doubts, worries and other negative thoughts, and to redirect your thoughts in a positive direction.

Regularly repeating these affirmations to yourself will remind you of the skills you have and help you believe that you can.

List the affirmations you plan to use during the walk/run program in the space provided.

Personal affirmations:

Combat negative thoughts and feelings

Sometimes you may have doubts about your ability or your progress. These negative thoughts can have a big impact on your feelings about yourself and your ability to accomplish your goals. Often these thoughts can be so powerful that you need to address them specifically. This is especially the case when you put yourself down, criticize your past actions, doubt your abilities and expect failure. Negative thinking can damage your self-confidence and your ability to begin and progress through a fitness program.

Some of your thoughts may be influencing how you see yourself and the world around you. There are a number of biased thinking patterns, and it can be helpful to know what they are so that you can challenge them if they arise.

Things are either black or white—never grey

You see things only in terms of right or wrong, good or bad, all or nothing, on or off. There is no middle ground for you. You might say to yourself:

- Either I follow the program exactly or I am quitting.
- If I don't find time for the program tomorrow, I'm finished with it.
- I only ran twice last week—I am failing.

Excuses, excuses, excuses

You blame the situation, the circumstances or others for your actions. You give your personal power away by believing you have no choice. You might say to yourself:

- If only my husband/wife were more active, then I would feel more motivated.
- The track/gym is too far away.
- It is too cold outside.

I should...

You expect perfection. You set unrealistic expectations and place demands on yourself that make you feel as if you are being forced to do something you do not really want to do. You might say to yourself:

- I should start this program.
- I should work out today.
- I should have been able to do the three workouts this week.

I don't measure up

You compare yourself with others and condemn yourself for not being the same or as good as them. You might say to yourself:

- Who am I kidding? I can never be like those people you see running.
- Everyone seems to go faster than I do. What is wrong with me? Why am I so slow?
- She looks a lot leaner than before we started this program, but I still look exactly the same. In fact, I think I have gained weight.

I am an idiot

You are the schoolyard bully to yourself. You make downright nasty and harsh comments about your progress, your body, how you look and anything else. You might say to yourself:

- There is no way I can do a program like that.
- I know that I will look stupid trying to do this.
- I am such a loser. What made me think I could try something like this?

What's the point?

You are frustrated with your progress or lack of it and ready to give up. Too many things have gone wrong or seem stacked against you. You might say to yourself:

- This is way too hard. I might as well forget about doing this program.
- Everything is going wrong. First I injured my ankle and now I have a cold. Why am I bothering with this?
- I can't do this anymore. I am just going to stop right now.

Some of these thoughts may sound very familiar to you and may have prevented you from achieving your fitness goals in the past. There are good reasons why negative thoughts are so powerful:

- They feel automatic. Your thoughts often seem as if they are spontaneous and that you have no control over them. You have learned them so well that they appear to arise involuntarily.
- You believe them. When you say things to yourself, you believe them without question or evaluation, no matter how crazy or distorted they may be.
- They are hard to shut out. Once negative thoughts arise, they take on a life of their own. Often they lead to other negative thoughts and it seems impossible to turn them off.

Despite the power of these thoughts and the negative feelings they can lead to, you can learn how to manage them. Here are four steps you can take to combat negative thoughts.

Step 1: Be aware of your thoughts

Observe your thoughts for a time to be aware of your thought patterns. What events trigger which thoughts, and how so these thoughts make you feel? Your beliefs about an event often end up leading to an undesirable consequence. This pattern is called the A-B-C pattern of thinking:

Action → Belief → Consequence

Consider the examples on the facing page.

ACTION	BELIEF	CONSEQUENCE
I start to think about beginning the walk/run program.	I don't know if I can. I am not really good with physical activity. It seems to come so easily to others.	I feel defeated, helpless, not in control, depressed.
January rolls around and I don't join the running clinic I planned to join.	I should join. I need to get fitter and healthier. If only one of my friends would join.	I feel guilty, resentful.

Step 2: Sound the alarm

Once you start to recognize your thought patterns, you can challenge your beliefs and try to change how you feel. You can begin by making yourself sit up and take notice when a negative thought strikes. Whenever you find yourself having a negative thought, sound a mental alarm and alert yourself to the situation. Make the alarm loud and meaningful. Some effective alarms are police/ambulance sirens and clock-radio buzzers. You could just say "stop" to yourself or have a stop sign posted where you need it, but sillier alarms can be more effective—an alarm that makes you smile disrupts your automatic response and allows you to step back from the situation before reacting. Find the alarm that works best for you.

Step 3: Challenge negative thoughts

Now that you have warned yourself about the negative thoughts, you can argue against them and try to change your feelings. Here are some questions you can use to help you through the process.

- Is it useful for me to have this thought?
- Is there a way to look at this situation differently?
- Am I thinking in a biased way?
- What evidence supports what I am thinking?
- How will I feel later if I listen and act on my thoughts right now?
- Will the negatives outweigh the positives if I give in now?

Take your beliefs, find a way to dispute them and imagine what the consequence might change. Consider the example below.

BELIEF	CHALLENGE DIALOGUE	NEW CONSEQUENCE
I don't know if I can. I am not really good with physical activity. It seems to come so easily to others.	Of course, it is going to be hard, but I have faced tougher things before in my life. I just need to take it at my own pace.	I feel more in control, confident, strong-minded.

Step 4: Edit your thoughts

You can learn to replace negative thoughts with positive ones. All the negative thoughts you might have about starting a walk/run program take away from your energy and make it harder to carry on.

Write down any negative thoughts you have about the program in the space provided and then turn them into positive statements that will help you achieve your goals. Post these somewhere and remember to sound the alarm to remind yourself that you need to challenge and edit negative thoughts.

Exercise: Replacing negatives with positives

NEGATIVE THOUGHT	POSITIVE STATEMENT
I've tried to stay with a running program before and each time I've failed.	Every time I begin a new exercise program I get closer to sticking with it for good.
It's impossible to fit this run into my already busy schedule.	I can take a little time for myself every day because I deserve it. I'm the one in control of my time.

Manage your feelings and stresses

Sometimes you may feel frustrated or anxious about your fitness program. Sometimes you may feel overwhelmed by stressful life events and daily hassles. These feelings can take away from your belief that you can achieve your fitness goals. Being able to manage your feelings can help you feel more in control and can give you the confidence to achieve your goals.

Take a moment to list the stressful things in your life and in your day right now.

Exercise: Cataloguing stresses

STRESSFUL THINGS IN MY LIFE: Moving. Changing jobs. New baby

_____

_____

_____

_____

STRESSFUL THINGS IN MY DAY: Waiting in grocery store lineup on my way to pick up kids. Being interrupted at a meeting.

_____

_____

_____

If you find you have trouble dealing with negative thoughts and feelings caused by training and life's stresses, try the following exercises once every day or every other day. You may also want to look into other relaxation techniques such as yoga, meditation and guided imagery.

Exercise: Relaxation script
Two-minute relax
1. Stand comfortably with your hands down by your side.
2. Breathe in and out slowly.
3. Now take a big deep breath and as you breathe in count to four.

4. Now very slowly let your breath out as you count to eight.
5. Try this three times in a row.
6. Now return to your regular breathing and the rest of your day.

Ten-minute relax

1. Find a comfortable place to sit or lie down.
2. Breathe in and out slowly.
3. Let yourself relax.
4. Breathe in slowly. Breathe out slowly. Breathe in slowly. Breathe out slowly.
5. As you breathe out the next three breaths, say to yourself: Relax . . . Relax . . . Relax.
6. Feel the relaxation spread through your body like a wave flowing over you. Start at your head—breathe in/out and relax your head. Now focus on your arms—breathe in/out and relax your arms. Now focus on your hands and fingers—breathe in/out, relax your hands and fingers. Now focus on your body—breathe in/out, relax your body. Focus on your legs—breathe in/out, relax your legs. Move all the way down to your toes—breathe in/out and relax your toes.
7. Allow your whole body to relax and feel warm and heavy. Now return to your regular breathing and the rest of your day.

Creating the right training environment

Your environment can exert a powerful influence on your thoughts, feelings and actions. Sometimes it can feel as if you are powerless against your environment and that it controls you rather than you controlling it. You will need to create an environment that supports your fitness goals. When thinking about your walking/running environment, consider your social support network, your workout cues at home and elsewhere, and your rewards program.

Establish a social support network

A social support network can be one of the most important ingredients in your walking/running success. Important people in your life can provide you with inspiration and encouragement. A training group or a couple of walking/running friends can provide you with motivation, energy and enjoyment. If you run with a group, your run leader can provide important support related specifically to your training needs.

Take a moment to evaluate the kind of support you are receiving and to decide if you need more support or can improve on the support you already receive. Sometimes the people in your life can offer better support if you let them know what you would like them to do and say. Consider the examples below and list your own.

Exercise: Evaluating support

SOURCE OF SUPPORT	HOW COULD SUPPORT BE IMPROVED?
Husband	On the days I don't feel like running he either nags me to go or doesn't seem to care. I will ask him to be more encouraging.
Walk/run leader/trainer	She is very supportive. She always asks me how I am doing and encourages me to take it at my own pace. No improvement needed.
Walking/running partner	She is so negative when we walk/run that it brings me down. I will ask her to be more positive and focus on what we are accomplishing.

_____

_____

_____

Place cues where you need them

Some situations challenge your actions more than others do. Placing meaningful cues in your environment can remind you of your fitness goals. The cues that can help trigger the response or action you would like may be verbal (inspirational quotations posted on your fridge or bathroom mirror), visual (a running magazine on your coffee table), or physical (the act of putting on your running shoes by the door).

Check off the items that apply to you below and list other cues you might use.

Exercise: Using cues to stay on track

WHERE	CHALLENGE	HELPFUL CUE
☐ At work	☐ Lunchtime arrives and I don't feel like going for my workout.	☐ Post a copy of my mission statement on my computer.
☐ At home immediately after work	☐ I arrive home from work and feel too tired to work out as planned.	☐ Have my workout gear ready to put on as soon as I get home.
		☐ Tape a picture of a fit and healthy person to my fridge.

Using cues to stay on track

WHERE	CHALLENGE	HELPFUL CUE

Create a rewards program

Rewards help reinforce your behaviour and can be very helpful at the beginning of your program. Decide how you are going to reward yourself for following through with each day or each week of your workouts. Find rewards that are meaningful and motivating. A reward might be a new piece of active wear, an afternoon at the beach, a ticket to a concert or a walk on a favourite trail. In the beginning, you might want to have a few more material rewards to help keep you focused. As your workouts become rewarding on their own, you may want to reward yourself less frequently with less material kinds of rewards—visiting a new park for your run.

Use the following chart to describe the rewards you plan for yourself over the first 13 weeks. Find the balance between different kinds of rewards and make them all something worth achieving.

Exercise: Reward schedule

Week 1 reward:

Week 2 reward:

Week 3 reward:

Week 4 reward:

Week 6 reward:

Week 9 reward:

Week 13 reward:

Pulling it all together: Your personal motivation plan

Knowing how to support your fitness goals is an essential part of making them happen. You have worked through a number of exercises that have identified ways to support your objectives. Now it is time to pull all these elements together in a personal motivation plan. Use all you have learned from completing the exercises in this chapter to elaborate on your plan below.

You will have the opportunity to modify your plan as you progress through the program and discover new things you need and elements that do not work well. Be patient. Even though your plan might not be perfect at the start, it is still your key to unlocking the personal motivation power within you.

Personal Motivation Plan

My reasons for training

_____

_____

My vision statement

_____

_____

My mission statement

_____

_____

Obstacles I might encounter and how I will overcome them

_____

_____

Affirmations to keep me going

_____

_____

Negative thoughts and feelings I might experience and how I
will deal with them

_____

_____

My social support network

_____

_____

My training cues

_____

_____

My rewards

_____

_____

I've always wanted to be somebody,

but I see now I should have

been more specific.

JANE WAGNER

THE WELL-MANAGED RUNNER

As well as getting a good start with a personal motivation plan, you will need to manage five key aspects of your walking/running life to achieve your fitness goals. To become a well-managed runner or walker, you must pay attention to:

- Your equipment
- Your overall health
- Your body and its response to activity
- Your mind and its role in the training program
- Your lifestyle choices

Equipment

For the most part, walking and running are fairly inexpensive activities. While you do not need a lot of equipment, you will need certain items to maintain your comfort level, keep your body healthy and facilitate your training.

Shoes The shoes you wear while training are your most important piece of equipment. They need to feel comfortable and meet the needs of your feet. Some people are flat-footed, others have high arches; some people have feet that roll out when they run, others have feet that roll in. Regardless of your needs, there is a shoe out there for you. The key is to shop at a store that specializes in walking/running shoes and employs experienced, professional staff who can help you make the right choice. Good shoes not only feel good—they protect you from injury.

Clothing Comfort and climate are the two chief considerations when choosing your running attire. Some materials are more likely to rub against your skin and cause irritation or blisters. Some materials, such as cotton, retain moisture from rain or sweat and can become heavy and uncomfortable. Other materials, such as certain synthetics, pull moisture away from your body and remain light and comfortable. Your clothes will play an important role in maintaining your body temperature in different weather conditions.

Accessories There are a number of accessories (water bottle, sports watch, reflective vest for nighttime activity, etc.) that can contribute to your comfort and safety as you head down the road.

Tips for managing your equipment needs

☐ Go shopping for shoes later in the day when your feet are usually slightly larger.

☐ When your shoes get dirty, wash them by hand and leave them by a heat source to dry. Don't put them in the washing machine or dryer.

☐ Keep track of the distance or amount of time that you log in your shoes. You should consider new shoes every 800 km or 100 hours.

☐ Wear shirts and shorts made of synthetic fabric, not cotton.

☐ Wear synthetic socks to prevent blisters.

- ☐ Dress in layers when training in cold weather.
- ☐ Wear a cap or hat made of synthetic material when you walk or run in cold weather. Take it off when you feel warm and put it back on when you feel cold.
- ☐ Carry a water bottle in a holder on your longer workouts and make sure you use it.
- ☐ Use a fanny pack or shoe pouch to carry a few essentials with you—identification, change for a pay phone, petroleum jelly.
- ☐ Consider using a heart rate monitor to determine how hard you are working during your training.

Health

Managing your health is a process that does not, unfortunately, always get the attention it deserves. Following a walk/run program and challenging yourself to achieve your fitness goals also means assessing and monitoring your physical condition, gauging your exertion levels, building recovery time into your week and attending to any injuries.

Physical condition If you are going to make training part of your weekly routine, you will need to be in good health. See your family doctor before starting a walk/run program if you have any concerns or if you have conditions that should be monitored during training, such as chest pain, high blood pressure, heart disease, joint pain, asthma, menstrual irregularities or pregnancy. Moreover, if you have concerns about your health at any point in your training program, see your doctor immediately.

Exertion You should monitor how hard you feel you are working each time you walk or run. Some days may seem more difficult than others and that is natural—your body needs time to adapt to the training. By monitoring your exertion you can modify your workouts as needed. Use the 10-point exertion scale that is included in your journal pages to measure how hard you are working. (See Chapter 4 for more detail.)

Rest and recovery When you are following the 13-week walk/run programs described in Appendix A and B, you should observe the rest and recovery days that are built into each week. These days will give your body time to adapt to your training. You will gradually become stronger and more efficient. Your recovery days can involve both passive rest (little activity) and more active rest (leisurely walking, easy cycling, gentle swimming).

Injuries Pay attention to your body. Pain is a warning sign that should not be ignored. Early identification and treatment of an injury will allow for minimal interruptions in your training.

Tips for managing your health

- ☐ Visit your family doctor if you have concerns about your health.
- ☐ Ask your doctor to monitor your health during the walk/run program if you are pregnant or have other conditions that might compromise your health.
- ☐ Take your heart rate during and after exercise to get a sense of how hard your body is working.
- ☐ Slow your pace down or stop and walk if your breathing becomes overly laboured or if you experience dizziness or nausea. You can always pick up your pace once you feel better.
- ☐ Listen to your body and make adjustments to your activity if:
  - Your muscles are sore. You notice changes in your mood, appetite or sleep patterns. You experience cold or flu-like symptoms.
- ☐ Promptly treat injuries with RICE:
  - **R**est the injured area until an accurate diagnosis can be made.
  - **I**ce for approximately 20 minutes (allowing approximately one hour in between icing treatments).
  - **C**ompress the area by applying an elastic bandage.
  - **E**levate the injured area above the level of the heart.

☐ Modify your training when you are injured or ill and return to activity slowly after an injury.

☐ Find alternative activities to do as you recover from your injury.

☐ Seek out as much information about your injury as possible.

Body

Managing your body during a walk/run program can involve a lot more than completing workouts each week. In addition to your workouts, you should pay attention to the way you warm up and cool down, how you walk or run, and other ways you might build flexibility, strength and general fitness. Take a balanced approach to the overall development of your body.

Warm-up and cool-down routines The walk/run program described in Appendix A starts you out slowly and realistically and very gradually increases the intensity of your training. You should approach each of your workouts in the same way, gradually building up to full exertion. Your warm-up should consist of a light 10- to 15-minute activity such as walking to get the blood flow going, followed by controlled dynamic stretching of your muscles (hamstring, hip flexor, calf and lower back) through a comfortable range of motion. Your cool-down should consist of gentle, static stretching of the same muscle groups holding each stretch for 15 to 30 seconds.

Technique It doesn't really matter what you look like when you walk or run, but it is important that you move in a way that feels relaxed, comfortable and, above all, normal to you. There are three principles of good form that may help you adapt your style and make it more efficient and more comfortable:

• Erect posture
• Proper alignment of body parts (that is, ears over shoulders over hips over heels)
• Relaxed shoulders, arms and hands

Flexibility and strength Good flexibility and balanced strength can help you improve your walking or running style and ability, reduce injures and enhance recovery. Flexibility and strength are specific for each joint in the body. Structural features such as muscles, tendons, ligaments and bones combine to limit a joint's range of motion. Furthermore, muscle weaknesses in one area can cause problems in others and promote instability in your joints. Consider promoting your flexibility with a regular stretching routine and/or a yoga class. Regarding strength training, there are various strategies and it is important to get some direction from experts before you start. Try your local fitness centre, YM/YWCA or gym.

Cross-training Engaging in a variety of activities, such as hiking, weight training and cycling, along with your walk/run program allows you to develop overall strength and fitness. This general development can help you become a better walker or runner as well. Moreover, cross-training will keep you motivated, reduce your risk of injury and increase your enjoyment of walking or running by providing you with a variety of activities rather than the same activity practised over and over again.

Tips for managing your body

☐ Develop a warm-up and cool-down routine and follow it consistently.

☐ Before you walk or run, spin on a stationary bike set for low tension for 10 minutes.

☐ Keep your torso tall and erect and make sure your feet point straight ahead as you walk or run.

☐ Keep your shoulders, arms and hands relaxed as you walk or run.

☐ Have a qualified trainer assess your strength and design an appropriate strength program for you to follow.

☐ Take a class on how to use an exercise ball. Ball exercises work on developing your core strength (strength in your stomach, lower back, gluts and hips).

☐ Take a yoga class to improve your flexibility.

☐ Stretch while you watch TV.

☐ Learn to in-line skate. It is a great cross-training activity.

☐ Try your workout in the water. Water running is a low-impact activity and a healthy alternative to your regular workout.

Mind

Keeping your mind healthy when you are starting a walk/run program can be a challenging task. Good mental management focuses on the little things you can do each day to help you stay focused and enjoy your workout.

Motivation Sometimes the most difficult part of a walk/run program is consistently getting yourself out the door. Use your personal motivation plan to deal with the obstacles you face each day. Keep track of new challenges as they arise and then modify your plan accordingly. Also, remember that celebrating your accomplishments can help you stay motivated.

Coping strategies for training Feeling uncomfortable when training, especially at the beginning, is a natural part of developing your fitness and progressing to the next level. Sometimes distracting yourself from what you are doing will help you deal with the difficulty; other times focusing specifically on what you are doing will help you meet the challenge. Whatever you do, make your training time as enjoyable as possible by incorporating strategies that keep your thoughts, images, feelings and focus positive and appropriate for you. Try different strategies until you find what works best for you.

"Race" day If you choose to enter a fun walk/run, you will find that the day of the event brings with it all sorts of feelings, thoughts and expectations. These elements can contribute to your mental preparation for the big moment or they can drain your energy. The key is to create a familiar and comfortable environment for yourself, both before and during the event, by being prepared, staying relaxed and positive, and following your routine and plan.

Tips for managing your mind
- ☐ Follow your personal motivation plan and revise it as necessary.
- ☐ Imagine how good you will feel after you go for your walk or run and use this image when you start to feel tired.
- ☐ Challenge your negative thoughts and edit what you say to yourself by replacing negative thoughts with positive statements, and by using affirmations or thoughts that are more helpful.
- ☐ Set goals for each workout. Make them as simple or as complex as you like, but focus on the process rather than time-oriented outcomes.
- ☐ While on your route, set small goals to break the course down into achievable sections: "Slow down after the next lamppost" or "Push until the end of this song."
- ☐ Think about pleasant things while you walk or run: Plan a party or your day, write a poem in your head, think of a song you like and try to remember all the words. If you are working out with friends, talk with them.
- ☐ Keep yourself positive and present. Develop a personal mantra that you can say to help you as you walk or run: "I can do this" or "Just relax and breathe" or "Smooth and easy."
- ☐ Periodically scan your body for tension or tightness as you run or walk. Release the tension by allowing different muscles to jiggle momentarily.
- ☐ During a walk/run event or workout, use creative imagery to see yourself crossing the finish line or being followed by a TV camera as you move along the course.

☐ Before a walk/run event, know the course and have an event plan. Know where the hills, the water stations and the toilets are. Make a plan for completing the event. This knowledge and planning will give you comfort and control, and will allow you to maximize your resources for the physical and mental demands of the day.

Lifestyle

Making healthy lifestyle choices—eating and drinking right, sleeping well, and coping with stress—takes knowledge, planning and commitment. By training regularly you are challenging yourself physically and mentally, and that means you must make healthier choices in all areas of your life.

Nutrition The three main components of good nutrition are variety, balance and moderation. Healthy eating is about regularly selecting a variety of foods from all the main food groups: grain products, vegetables and fruits, dairy products, meat and alternatives. Ultimately, you also want to achieve an optimal balance of carbohydrates, fats and proteins. A 55-30-15 ratio is a good goal (that is, 55 per cent of your calories should come from carbohydrates, 30 per cent from fats and 15 per cent from proteins). Carbohydrates are an important fuel source for active people, but as a walker/runner you should remember that carbohydrates come from fruits and vegetables as well as grain products and you should increase your consumption of these alternative carbohydrate sources. You should also make sure you understand what exactly constitutes a serving and how many servings per day are recommended for each food group.

Hydration Drinking eight glasses of water a day is essential for optimal athletic performance. On days when you are training, you might want to drink more than eight glasses. Water is the main component of sweat, which helps cool you down. Water also helps you avoid unnecessary fatigue and potentially life-threatening conditions. Make sure you are properly hydrated at all times. If you wait to drink only when you are thirsty, you are already dehydrated.

Sleep Getting a good night's sleep is essential when you are taxing your body, yet sleep is one of the most neglected areas of lifestyle management. Not getting enough sleep affects your fatigue levels, mood and focus. It also makes you more susceptible to colds, flu and other illnesses. The amount of sleep each person needs will vary. Some people need only six hours while others may need ten hours. Listen to your body, find the right amount of sleep for you and make sleep-time a priority, especially when the signs are telling you that you should.

Stress A certain amount of stress in your life helps you function. However, too much stress for too long can take its toll on your body. Learn to be sensitive to the obvious and the subtle signs of stress in your life. If you have been feeling fatigued or irritable, have not been sleeping well or have noticed changes in your appetite, it is probably best to modify your schedule and find ways to relax. (See the relaxation exercises in Chapter 1.) Be aware of the stresses in your life, as these can have both an immediate and a cumulative effect on your health and well-being. Major life events and daily hassles can have a fairly significant impact on your thoughts, feelings and actions. When you are using the journal pages, you may find it helpful to record these kinds of stresses.

Tips for managing your lifestyle
☐ Plan your meals and snacks for the week. Take your plan to the grocery store and use it when you shop.
☐ Eat more fruits and vegetables every day.
☐ Rather than three large meals a day, eat smaller meals every two or three hours.
☐ Use monounsaturated fats such as olive and canola oil.

☐ Keep nutritious, lower-fat foods (carrots, raisins, an apple, a bagel) handy so that when you are hungry you will have a healthy snack available.

☐ Drink at least eight glasses of water a day.

☐ Drink at least two glasses of water two hours before exercise and one to three glasses after exercise.

☐ Get at least eight hours of sleep a night.

☐ Monitor your life stresses and daily stresses to gain an awareness of how they might be affecting your thoughts, feelings and focus.

☐ Take two to ten minutes each day to relax.

For too long I used the finish line as a

measure of my accomplishment. . . .

I am more inclined to view it as a confirmation

of my commitment to myself and the sport.

JOHN "THE PENGUIN" BINGHAM

MAKING THE COMMITMENT

Deciding that you want to start a walk/run program is the first step in making a commitment to yourself. Several factors, including your fitness goals, will help you determine the right level of commitment for you. Once you decide on the level of your commitment, you will be better able to make changes and accept the sacrifices necessary. Commitment is only possible when you know what is required, make plans and set realistic goals.

Understanding the walk/run program time requirements

Before you make your commitment, you need to know exactly what you are committing to. The walk/run program described in Appendix A is 13 weeks long. There are three workouts each week and each workout lasts from 35 to 66 minutes.

You will need to look at your schedule and find blocks of time to accommodate the workouts shown below. (See Appendix A for the complete training schedule.)

Time needed for the walk/run program

Week	Session 1	Session 2	Session 3
1	35 minutes	40 minutes	40 minutes
2	45 minutes	40 minutes	40 minutes
3	50 minutes	40 minutes	50 minutes
4	55 minutes	45 minutes	50 minutes
5	60 minutes	50 minutes	50 minutes
6	65 minutes	50 minutes	55 minutes
7	60 minutes	54 minutes	54 minutes
8	60 minutes	48 minutes	54 minutes
9	63 minutes	54 minutes	50 minutes
10	44 minutes	41 minutes	45 minutes
11	51 minutes	56 minutes	51 minutes
12	66 minutes	66 minutes	45 minutes
13	50 minutes	40 minutes	60 minutes

Finding the time

Life is a balancing act, and it can be hard to find time for every-thing. At different points in your life you will have different pri-orities and these priorities will be reflected in the choices you make. However, it is always easy to spend too much time on one area (for instance, work) and neglect other areas (for instance, fitness) when you become too busy.

Initially, when you are considering making a commitment to something like a walk/run program, it can help to examine the different areas of life (work, family, hobbies, etc.) that you are trying to keep in balance. How much time can you realistically allow for each area? What areas are the most important to you?

Begin by thinking about the total amount of time you have available as a "pie" that can be divided into so many pieces of different sizes. For example:

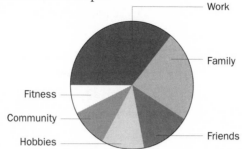

Take a moment to identify the important areas of your life, then divide the pie below into as many sections as you need for these areas. Label each section and use your completed pie to think about ways you can make time for three workouts each week.

My time and how I spend it

Once you have this image of your time and how you use it, you can see if it aligns with your priorities in life. Sometimes you can rework your schedule to make room for the areas that you feel are being shortchanged. This is something you may have to do to achieve your fitness goals.

Make your workout part of your daily routine
There are a number of things you can do to incorporate a workout into your day. Before you start training, you might want to try a "dry" week of workouts. Imagine yourself working out at particular points over the course of the week. This can help you identify blocks of time and can also get you ready mentally to start the program. You can then think about the following scheduling tips.

Schedule your workout. Set a specific time for your workout. If it is not specific, it can be easily overlooked or neglected.

Schedule your workout earlier in the day. If your workout is in the morning, you are more likely to do it—workouts scheduled at the end of the day can get bumped from your schedule by other activities.

Minimize obstacles. The more you have to do (pick up groceries, mow the lawn, feed the cat, etc.) before going for your workout, the more likely you are to miss your walk or run. Try to make the path to your workout as short and as free of obstacles as possible.

Have an alternate plan. Things often come up unexpectedly. Be realistic and flexible. Have another time when you can do your workout, but only use your alternate time when you really need to.

Substitute your workout for another activity. Perhaps you usually watch your son or daughter's 60-minute soccer practice, or you sit and read the paper and have a coffee every day in the morning, or maybe you go for a drink after work. It may be possible to substitute your workout for one of these activities.

Remember you only need to find three blocks of about 60 minutes each week.

Be creative with your time. Look for time where there appears to be none. For example, if you are looking after your children during the day, start a workout/play group. Half the adults can look after the children while the other half go for a workout and then you can switch.

Now use the chart below to schedule your workouts. Be specific about what you do each day. Schedule your workouts and alternative workout times. Try to treat your workout as an appointment with yourself that you can't miss.

MY WEEK	MORNING	AFTERNOON	EVENING
Monday			
Tuesday			
Wednesday			
Thursday			
Friday			
Saturday			
Sunday			

Setting goals

Setting goals involves identifying what you want to achieve in very specific terms. As you get ready to start a walk/run program, you will need both long-term program goals and short-term weekly action goals. At different points in the program you will be prompted to revisit your program goals, your action goals and your personal motivation plan to see if you need to make any changes to help you along the way. You should feel free to revisit and adjust your goals as often as necessary. And whether you are setting or adjusting goals, you should make sure that they are smart: Specific, Measurable, Adjustable, Realistic, Time-based.

Specific goals are more effective. Clearly outline what you want to achieve along with how you plan to achieve it.

Measurable goals let you know when you have achieved your goal or how far you still have to go. Identify exactly how you will know when you have achieved your goal.

Adjustable goals help you avoid frustration. Make your goals flexible and easy to modify rather than rigid, and refine them as necessary based on your life's demands and your progress.

Realistic goals are neither impossible to achieve nor too easy. Maintain your motivation by challenging yourself, but do so at a reasonable pace that allows you to achieve your goals within the allotted time frame.

Time-based goals allow you to focus and allocate your time and resources. Decide exactly when you want to achieve your goal. Avoid setting a time that is too vague (e.g., "a few weeks from now") or too far in the future.

Setting SMART goals takes practice, but in time you should be able to develop a good sense of the process.

Set program goals

The Beginning Runner's Journal is organized in a way that will help you set manageable program goals. The 26 weeks of journal pages are divided into two 13-week blocks. You can set your program goals for the first 13 weeks and then follow the same procedure for the second 13 weeks. Your program goals will give you something to work towards and help you stay motivated and focused on achieving your overall fitness goals. You might like to begin by referring to the exercises you completed in Chapter 1 or to the tips for becoming a well-managed runner in Chapter 2.

Decide what you would like to achieve in the first 13-week period and list your goals in the space provided. As well, define end points related to your program goals—how you will know when you have met your goals.

Sample

My program goals for the first 13 weeks:

- *Follow the walk/run program requirements.*
- *Use my personal motivation plan to help me stay on track.*
- *Eat at least three servings of fruits and vegetables each day.*

I will know that I have met my program goals when:

- *I work out three times a week consistently.*
- *I am able to overcome my negative self-talk and other obstacles.*
- *I am eating at least three servings of fruits and vegetables regularly.*

Date I would like to achieve these goals by (13 weeks from when I start): *April 24*

My program goals for the first 13 weeks:

_____

_____

I will know that I have met my program goals when:

_____

_____

Date I would like to achieve these goals by (13 weeks from when I start):

_____

_____

Set action goals

Short-term action goals refer to the specific actions you must take in a particular week to maintain your workout schedule and move towards your program goals. The actions are more process-oriented than outcome-oriented. The actions will change from week to week as you learn about yourself and identify different challenges. They are more specific, flexible and relevant than your program goals. Therefore, you should only identify them immediately before the week starts or during the week itself.

Try to outline some action goals for the first week of your program.

Sample

Short-term action goals:

- _Schedule my three workouts before the week starts._
- _Repeat my affirmations at breakfast, lunch and dinner._
- _Do at least one of my workouts with Brenda this week to ensure that I go._
- _Shop for vegetables and fruit._

Short-term action goals (for Week 1):

_____

_____

Focusing on the process

Progress takes time and rarely occurs in a consistently forward or upward fashion. In fact, the road to improvement is similar to your walk/run route—there are a number of ups and downs along the way. You should strive to maintain a positive perspective and focus on the process.

Learn from your experiences and setbacks. Each week you are going to learn something about yourself, but only if you choose to do so. See every experience as a learning opportunity and do not judge yourself by the outcome alone. Setbacks are part of the process. There are going to be times when you cannot stick to your training schedule because of illness, injury or other pressures. However, within each of these experiences there are valuable lessons. Maybe you started training too hard and got injured, or maybe you planned your workout for the end of the day and never had time to get to it. Your experiences can teach you about your patterns of responding and they can help you identify the elements you need to change to reach your goals. Don't dismiss your setbacks—challenge yourself to learn from them.

Keep track of your highlights and accomplishments. List your highlights and accomplishments in your journal and celebrate them. They can be as simple as a satisfying workout with a friend or as rewarding as a burst of energy during your workout. Circle your highlights and accomplishments as you review the week in your journal. Remember that these successes contribute to your belief in yourself, your ability and your potential.

Make the change. To grow and develop, you need to apply the lessons you learn and make the necessary changes in your life. Nike coined "Just Do It"—a slogan that has a lot of merit when it comes to making personal changes. Change is all about action. No one can make the change for you. So try something different or new. Step outside your comfort zone and challenge yourself.

Committing to a personal lifestyle contract

The final step in making the commitment to a walk/run program involves a personal lifestyle contract that describes the choices and changes before you and how you intend to respond to them. The contract provided here outlines what you need to do each day to achieve your fitness potential. It also includes space for any other commitments you wish to make.

When you are thinking about committing to a personal lifestyle contract, remember that the road is challenging, but the rewards are plentiful.

Personal Lifestyle Contract

I, _____ vow to:

☐ Make the necessary choices to achieve my fitness goals.

☐ Attempt to get better at my motivation every day.

☐ Try new things and challenge myself every day.

☐ Make the time to achieve my fitness potential.

☐ Embrace any setbacks I have and learn from them.

☐ _____

☐ _____

☐ _____

Signed: _____ Date: _____

All people who excel are masters at

drawing lessons from their experiences.

Without ongoing reflection and assessment

there is little chance of ongoing growth.

TERRY ORLICK

USING THE JOURNAL PAGES

When you have completed a personal motivation plan, set some program goals and made a commitment to yourself and your fitness vision, you are ready to begin a walk/run program and start recording your experiences and accomplishments.

The Beginning Runner's Journal contains pages for 26 weeks of journal entries. The pages are divided into two 13-week blocks, and each block includes space for reviewing your experience at the 6-week and 13-week points.

After you write about the first 13-week program, you will have an opportunity to learn from your experiences before moving on to write about a second 13-week program. At this point you can make adjustments to your personal motivation plan and reset your fitness goals. You can also decide on the program you want to follow for the next 13 weeks—a continuation of the walk/run program you have just tried (Appendix A), the walk/run maintenance program (Appendix B) or another training program offered in your community. The program you choose for the second 13 weeks is up to you. Challenge yourself to extend your training experience beyond six months so that it becomes an established part of your routine.

Be consistent

Choose a regular time to write in your journal, perhaps right before you go to bed. Try to write every day, even when you don't have a scheduled walk or run. Tracking all of your activities can be useful. The journal pages are easy to use and provide you with space to:

- Record your activities and actions
- Rate elements of your day
- Rate the intensity of your workout
- Comment generally on your thoughts and experiences

Through consistent writing and monitoring, you will be able to examine yourself more objectively and start to see ways to change and improve as you move towards your ultimate fitness potential.

Activities and actions

Use this space to describe your activities for the day and the actions you took to support your goals. On the days you walk or run, simply record the specifics along with any other activities you undertook (e.g., walked home from work, took the stairs instead of the elevator, gardened). On the days you do not formally work out, record your activities or actions as well. Your actions can relate to your fitness goals, your personal motivation plan or the tips in Chapter 2.

Sample for a day with a workout

- *40 minutes: Ran 30 seconds. Walked 4 minutes and 30 seconds. (8 times).*

- *Went straight to the track after work and met Brenda to do the workout.*
- *Drank 8 glasses of water over the day.*

Sample for a day without a workout
- *Gardened for an hour.*
- *Went to bed early because I was feeling tired.*
- *Iced my ankle because it was a little sore.*

How I felt?
Use the 5-point scale in this section to rate how you felt physically, mentally, about your nutrition and about your sleep.

1 = Poor
2 = Below average
3 = Average
4 = Above average
5 = Excellent

Some days are going to be more challenging than others for various reasons (e.g., you may feel "below average" physically as your body gets used to the training load, or "poor" mentally because of stressful events in your life). Monitoring your body, mind, nutrition and sleep can help you identify the factors contributing to your good and bad days. Sometimes you can even modify your activities and actions based on your ratings (e.g., you can push yourself a little harder on a workout if you notice you have been feeling particularly good, or you can go to bed earlier if you notice you haven't been sleeping well). The scales are quick and easy to complete and, if you are motivated, you can graph your feelings in each area over the course of a week or month.

How hard did I work?
Use the 10-point scale in this section to rate your exertion level during your walk or run.

1 "This is easy." Breathing easy, no fatigue
2 Breathing easy, sweating very lightly, no fatigue
3 Aware of breath but still easy, muscles warming up, sweating lightly, no fatigue
4 Breathing slightly elevated, muscles warm, sweating, can carry on a conversation, slight fatigue
5 A little breathless, muscles working, sweating more, a little more fatigue
6 Breathing harder and deeper, can still hold a conversation, increase in fatigue but can keep going for a while
7 Breathing hard and deep and aware of it, can still talk but would prefer not to, definite fatigue
8 Breathing laboured, can only grunt in answer to questions, very definite fatigue
9 Breathing very laboured, no talking possible, cannot maintain for very long, overwhelming fatigue
10 "This is ridiculous." Breathing extremely laboured, ready to stop at any time, all-out fatigue

The first few weeks will be tough as your body adapts to the training load and you may rate some or all of the workouts as 8 or higher. However, as you become fitter, the workouts will seem a little easier or you will notice that you can work harder for longer. Monitoring your exertion levels can help you find a balance between pushing yourself too hard and not challenging yourself enough. By paying attention to your body, you will be able to modify your pace as necessary and understand the factors that are making the workout feel easy or hard. This scale can also give you an indication of your fitness improvements.

Notes and reflections
Use this space to describe your experience of training or your day in more detail. You can focus your writing on your activities

and actions, or you can describe other aspects of your day—feelings during your workout, social support you enjoyed, highlights, obstacles you overcame, moods, thoughts and things you can improve or change. You decide what you want to reflect on here. These daily notes provide valuable information that can help you modify your personal motivation plan and your fitness goals and learn from your experiences. The more time you spend on these, the more you will gain.

Sample

- *I thought I wasn't going to get my workout in today because of all the other things I had to do, so it was great that I had arranged to meet Brenda. She is so good to run with. I was a little tired at first, but then I got into it. Plus I felt so good afterwards and more focused when I went back to work. I wonder if we could run together twice a week instead of only once.*

Highlights and accomplishments this week

Use this space to record events and milestones worth celebrating. If you are unable to identify many highlights, then perhaps you need to find ways to increase your opportunities for fun and success. Remember, the program is not all about outcome. If you are not enjoying what you are doing, then you will find it hard to stay motivated and achieve your goals.

Sample

- *I ran at the beach on Wednesday. It was so beautiful. I just took it nice and easy on the run and soaked up the day.*
- *I had a crazy, busy Friday and normally I would miss my lunchtime workout, but this week I did it!*

Actions for next week

Use this space to identify actions that will help you maintain your workout schedule and move towards your program goals in the week ahead. These short-term action goals should reflect the lessons you have learned from the previous week, and they should relate specifically to the challenges of the next week.

Sample

- *Run with Brenda twice.*
- *Write my workout times in my day planner.*
- *Take a few more healthy snacks with me during the day (carrots, apple).*

Week 6 review

Six weeks after you start each 13-week training block, use this space to assess your progress. Briefly review how you are doing and answer the questions included. Take the opportunity to make changes to your personal motivation plan or program goals. Identify other short-term action goals that can help you continue with the program.

Week 13 review

When you reach the end of each 13-week training block, use this space to assess your experience overall. Reflect on your experience and answer the questions included. If you are continuing with training, take the opportunity to make changes to your personal motivation plan and program goals.

Don't let missed days and weeks stop you

There will be some days or even weeks when you do not record your activities. Don't get caught up in feeling guilty about these gaps, and certainly don't use them as an excuse to stop writing. Instead, turn these missed days and weeks into opportunities to learn about yourself. When you get a chance, explain *why* you missed recording a particular day or week so that when you go back to review your experience you can identify actions you might take in the future.

This journal is all about you and your journey to make fitness a regular part of your life—make it as complete as possible but accept that a hectic schedule will sometimes make you miss an entry or two.

Good luck!

WEEK 1

MONDAY · DATE:

Activities/Actions:

| **How I felt:** | Physically | 1 2 3 4 5 | About my nutrition | 1 2 3 4 5 |
| | Mentally | 1 2 3 4 5 | About my sleep | 1 2 3 4 5 |

How hard did I work?   1   2   3   4   5   6   7   8   9   10

Notes and reflections:

TUESDAY · DATE:

Activities/Actions:

| **How I felt:** | Physically | 1 2 3 4 5 | About my nutrition | 1 2 3 4 5 |
| | Mentally | 1 2 3 4 5 | About my sleep | 1 2 3 4 5 |

How hard did I work?   1   2   3   4   5   6   7   8   9   10

Notes and reflections:

WEDNESDAY · DATE:

Activities/Actions:

| How I felt: | Physically | 1 2 3 4 5 | About my nutrition | 1 2 3 4 5 |
| | Mentally | 1 2 3 4 5 | About my sleep | 1 2 3 4 5 |

How hard did I work?   1   2   3   4   5   6   7   8   9   10

Notes and reflections:

THURSDAY · DATE:

Activities/Actions:

| How I felt: | Physically | 1 2 3 4 5 | About my nutrition | 1 2 3 4 5 |
| | Mentally | 1 2 3 4 5 | About my sleep | 1 2 3 4 5 |

How hard did I work?   1   2   3   4   5   6   7   8   9   10

Notes and reflections:

FRIDAY · DATE:

Activities/Actions:

| **How I felt:** | Physically | 1 2 3 4 5 | About my nutrition | 1 2 3 4 5 |
| | Mentally | 1 2 3 4 5 | About my sleep | 1 2 3 4 5 |

How hard did I work?   1   2   3   4   5   6   7   8   9   10

Notes and reflections:

SATURDAY · DATE:

Activities/Actions:

| **How I felt:** | Physically | 1 2 3 4 5 | About my nutrition | 1 2 3 4 5 |
| | Mentally | 1 2 3 4 5 | About my sleep | 1 2 3 4 5 |

How hard did I work?   1   2   3   4   5   6   7   8   9   10

Notes and reflections:

SUNDAY · DATE:

Activities/Actions:

| **How I felt:** | Physically | 1 2 3 4 5 | About my nutrition | 1 2 3 4 5 |
| | Mentally | 1 2 3 4 5 | About my sleep | 1 2 3 4 5 |

How hard did I work?   1   2   3   4   5   6   7   8   9   10

Notes and reflections:

Highlights/accomplishments for the week:

Actions for next week:

WEEK 2

MONDAY · DATE:

Activities/Actions:

How I felt: Physically 1 2 3 4 5   About my nutrition 1 2 3 4 5

Mentally 1 2 3 4 5   About my sleep 1 2 3 4 5

How hard did I work? 1 2 3 4 5 6 7 8 9 10

Notes and reflections:

TUESDAY · DATE:

Activities/Actions:

How I felt: Physically 1 2 3 4 5   About my nutrition 1 2 3 4 5

Mentally 1 2 3 4 5   About my sleep 1 2 3 4 5

How hard did I work? 1 2 3 4 5 6 7 8 9 10

Notes and reflections:

WEDNESDAY · DATE:

Activities/Actions:

| **How I felt:** | Physically | 1 2 3 4 5 | About my nutrition | 1 2 3 4 5 |
| | Mentally | 1 2 3 4 5 | About my sleep | 1 2 3 4 5 |

How hard did I work? 1 2 3 4 5 6 7 8 9 10

Notes and reflections:

THURSDAY · DATE:

Activities/Actions:

| **How I felt:** | Physically | 1 2 3 4 5 | About my nutrition | 1 2 3 4 5 |
| | Mentally | 1 2 3 4 5 | About my sleep | 1 2 3 4 5 |

How hard did I work? 1 2 3 4 5 6 7 8 9 10

Notes and reflections:

FRIDAY · DATE:

Activities/Actions:

| **How I felt:** | Physically | 1 2 3 4 5 | About my nutrition | 1 2 3 4 5 |
| | Mentally | 1 2 3 4 5 | About my sleep | 1 2 3 4 5 |

How hard did I work?   1   2   3   4   5   6   7   8   9   10

Notes and reflections:

SATURDAY · DATE:

Activities/Actions:

| **How I felt:** | Physically | 1 2 3 4 5 | About my nutrition | 1 2 3 4 5 |
| | Mentally | 1 2 3 4 5 | About my sleep | 1 2 3 4 5 |

How hard did I work?   1   2   3   4   5   6   7   8   9   10

Notes and reflections:

SUNDAY · DATE:

Activities/Actions:

| How I felt: | Physically | 1 2 3 4 5 | About my nutrition | 1 2 3 4 5 |
| | Mentally | 1 2 3 4 5 | About my sleep | 1 2 3 4 5 |

How hard did I work? 1 2 3 4 5 6 7 8 9 10

Notes and reflections:

Highlights/accomplishments for the week:

Actions for next week:

WEEK 3

MONDAY · DATE:

Activities/Actions:

How I felt: Physically   1   2   3   4   5   About my nutrition   1   2   3   4   5

         Mentally   1   2   3   4   5   About my sleep   1   2   3   4   5

How hard did I work?   1   2   3   4   5   6   7   8   9   10

Notes and reflections:

TUESDAY · DATE:

Activities/Actions:

How I felt: Physically   1   2   3   4   5   About my nutrition   1   2   3   4   5

         Mentally   1   2   3   4   5   About my sleep   1   2   3   4   5

How hard did I work?   1   2   3   4   5   6   7   8   9   10

Notes and reflections:

WEDNESDAY · DATE:

Activities/Actions:

| **How I felt:** | Physically | 1 2 3 4 5 | About my nutrition | 1 2 3 4 5 |
| | Mentally | 1 2 3 4 5 | About my sleep | 1 2 3 4 5 |

How hard did I work? 1 2 3 4 5 6 7 8 9 10

Notes and reflections:

THURSDAY · DATE:

Activities/Actions:

| **How I felt:** | Physically | 1 2 3 4 5 | About my nutrition | 1 2 3 4 5 |
| | Mentally | 1 2 3 4 5 | About my sleep | 1 2 3 4 5 |

How hard did I work? 1 2 3 4 5 6 7 8 9 10

Notes and reflections:

FRIDAY · DATE:

Activities/Actions:

| How I felt: | Physically | 1 2 3 4 5 | About my nutrition | 1 2 3 4 5 |
| | Mentally | 1 2 3 4 5 | About my sleep | 1 2 3 4 5 |

How hard did I work?   1   2   3   4   5   6   7   8   9   10

Notes and reflections:

SATURDAY · DATE:

Activities/Actions:

| How I felt: | Physically | 1 2 3 4 5 | About my nutrition | 1 2 3 4 5 |
| | Mentally | 1 2 3 4 5 | About my sleep | 1 2 3 4 5 |

How hard did I work?   1   2   3   4   5   6   7   8   9   10

Notes and reflections:

SUNDAY · DATE:

Activities/Actions:

How I felt:	Physically	1 2 3 4 5	About my nutrition	1 2 3 4 5
	Mentally	1 2 3 4 5	About my sleep	1 2 3 4 5

How hard did I work?   1   2   3   4   5   6   7   8   9   10

Notes and reflections:

Highlights/accomplishments for the week:

Actions for next week:

WEEK 4

MONDAY · DATE:

Activities/Actions:

| **How I felt:** | Physically | 1 2 3 4 5 | About my nutrition | 1 2 3 4 5 |
| | Mentally | 1 2 3 4 5 | About my sleep | 1 2 3 4 5 |

How hard did I work?   1   2   3   4   5   6   7   8   9   10

Notes and reflections:

TUESDAY · DATE:

Activities/Actions:

| **How I felt:** | Physically | 1 2 3 4 5 | About my nutrition | 1 2 3 4 5 |
| | Mentally | 1 2 3 4 5 | About my sleep | 1 2 3 4 5 |

How hard did I work?   1   2   3   4   5   6   7   8   9   10

Notes and reflections:

WEDNESDAY · DATE:

Activities/Actions:

| **How I felt:** | Physically | 1 2 3 4 5 | About my nutrition | 1 2 3 4 5 |
| | Mentally | 1 2 3 4 5 | About my sleep | 1 2 3 4 5 |

How hard did I work? 1 2 3 4 5 6 7 8 9 10

Notes and reflections:

THURSDAY · DATE:

Activities/Actions:

| **How I felt:** | Physically | 1 2 3 4 5 | About my nutrition | 1 2 3 4 5 |
| | Mentally | 1 2 3 4 5 | About my sleep | 1 2 3 4 5 |

How hard did I work? 1 2 3 4 5 6 7 8 9 10

Notes and reflections:

FRIDAY · DATE:

Activities/Actions:

| **How I felt:** | Physically | 1 2 3 4 5 | About my nutrition | 1 2 3 4 5 |
| | Mentally | 1 2 3 4 5 | About my sleep | 1 2 3 4 5 |

How hard did I work?   1   2   3   4   5   6   7   8   9   10

Notes and reflections:

SATURDAY · DATE:

Activities/Actions:

| **How I felt:** | Physically | 1 2 3 4 5 | About my nutrition | 1 2 3 4 5 |
| | Mentally | 1 2 3 4 5 | About my sleep | 1 2 3 4 5 |

How hard did I work?   1   2   3   4   5   6   7   8   9   10

Notes and reflections:

SUNDAY · DATE:

Activities/Actions:

How I felt:	Physically	1 2 3 4 5	About my nutrition	1 2 3 4 5
	Mentally	1 2 3 4 5	About my sleep	1 2 3 4 5

How hard did I work?   1   2   3   4   5   6   7   8   9   10

Notes and reflections:

Highlights/accomplishments for the week:

Actions for next week:

WEEK 5

MONDAY · DATE:

Activities/Actions:

How I felt: Physically   1   2   3   4   5   About my nutrition   1   2   3   4   5

          Mentally   1   2   3   4   5   About my sleep   1   2   3   4   5

How hard did I work?   1   2   3   4   5   6   7   8   9   10

Notes and reflections:

TUESDAY · DATE:

Activities/Actions:

How I felt: Physically   1   2   3   4   5   About my nutrition   1   2   3   4   5

          Mentally   1   2   3   4   5   About my sleep   1   2   3   4   5

How hard did I work?   1   2   3   4   5   6   7   8   9   10

Notes and reflections:

WEDNESDAY · DATE:

Activities/Actions:

How I felt: Physically	1	2	3	4	5	About my nutrition	1	2	3	4	5
Mentally	1	2	3	4	5	About my sleep	1	2	3	4	5

How hard did I work?   1   2   3   4   5   6   7   8   9   10

Notes and reflections:

THURSDAY · DATE:

Activities/Actions:

How I felt: Physically	1	2	3	4	5	About my nutrition	1	2	3	4	5
Mentally	1	2	3	4	5	About my sleep	1	2	3	4	5

How hard did I work?   1   2   3   4   5   6   7   8   9   10

Notes and reflections:

FRIDAY · DATE:

Activities/Actions:

How I felt: Physically 1 2 3 4 5   About my nutrition 1 2 3 4 5

Mentally 1 2 3 4 5   About my sleep 1 2 3 4 5

How hard did I work? 1 2 3 4 5 6 7 8 9 10

Notes and reflections:

SATURDAY · DATE:

Activities/Actions:

How I felt: Physically 1 2 3 4 5   About my nutrition 1 2 3 4 5

Mentally 1 2 3 4 5   About my sleep 1 2 3 4 5

How hard did I work? 1 2 3 4 5 6 7 8 9 10

Notes and reflections:

SUNDAY · DATE:

Activities/Actions:

| **How I felt:** | Physically | 1 2 3 4 5 | About my nutrition | 1 2 3 4 5 |
| | Mentally | 1 2 3 4 5 | About my sleep | 1 2 3 4 5 |

How hard did I work? 1 2 3 4 5 6 7 8 9 10

Notes and reflections:

Highlights/accomplishments for the week:

Actions for next week:

WEEK 6

MONDAY · DATE:

Activities/Actions:

How I felt: Physically	1 2 3 4 5	About my nutrition	1 2 3 4 5
Mentally	1 2 3 4 5	About my sleep	1 2 3 4 5

How hard did I work?　1　2　3　4　5　6　7　8　9　10

Notes and reflections:

TUESDAY · DATE:

Activities/Actions:

How I felt: Physically	1 2 3 4 5	About my nutrition	1 2 3 4 5
Mentally	1 2 3 4 5	About my sleep	1 2 3 4 5

How hard did I work?　1　2　3　4　5　6　7　8　9　10

Notes and reflections:

WEDNESDAY · DATE:

Activities/Actions:

| **How I felt:** Physically | 1 2 3 4 5 | About my nutrition | 1 2 3 4 5 |
| Mentally | 1 2 3 4 5 | About my sleep | 1 2 3 4 5 |

How hard did I work?   1   2   3   4   5   6   7   8   9   10

Notes and reflections:

THURSDAY · DATE:

Activities/Actions:

| **How I felt:** Physically | 1 2 3 4 5 | About my nutrition | 1 2 3 4 5 |
| Mentally | 1 2 3 4 5 | About my sleep | 1 2 3 4 5 |

How hard did I work?   1   2   3   4   5   6   7   8   9   10

Notes and reflections:

FRIDAY · DATE:

Activities/Actions:

How I felt: Physically 1 2 3 4 5   About my nutrition 1 2 3 4 5
Mentally 1 2 3 4 5   About my sleep 1 2 3 4 5

How hard did I work? 1   2   3   4   5   6   7   8   9   10

Notes and reflections:

SATURDAY · DATE:

Activities/Actions:

How I felt: Physically 1 2 3 4 5   About my nutrition 1 2 3 4 5
Mentally 1 2 3 4 5   About my sleep 1 2 3 4 5

How hard did I work? 1   2   3   4   5   6   7   8   9   10

Notes and reflections:

SUNDAY · DATE:

Activities/Actions:

How I felt:	Physically	1 2 3 4 5	About my nutrition	1 2 3 4 5
	Mentally	1 2 3 4 5	About my sleep	1 2 3 4 5

How hard did I work?   1   2   3   4   5   6   7   8   9   10

Notes and reflections:

Highlights/accomplishments for the week:

Actions for next week:

Congratulations! You have completed the first six weeks of the walk/run program. Briefly examine your journal entries for the past six weeks and answer the following questions.

1. What were the main highlights of the past six weeks? What were your biggest accomplishments?
2. How have you been celebrating your accomplishments?
3. What were your biggest challenges of the past six weeks?
4. Which of your actions have moved you towards your goals or helped you overcome obstacles?
5. Which of your actions have not been helpful or have discouraged you?
6. Has anything happened that you did not expect?
7. What actions do you need to focus on over the next seven weeks to help you through the process?

Now consider your personal motivation plan and how it has been working for you. What actions could you take to improve the following parts of your plan?

Vision/Mission

Handling obstacles

Thoughts and feelings

Social support

Cues in the environment

Rewards

Describe your goals for the week ahead (Week 7).

Short-term action goals:

_____

_____

_____

Take a moment to write anything you would like in this space. You can reflect further on your experience with the walk/run program or examine other aspects of your life right now.

Thoughts and reflections:

_____

_____

_____

_____

_____

_____

_____

_____

WEEK 7

MONDAY · DATE:

Activities/Actions:

How I felt: Physically   1   2   3   4   5   About my nutrition   1   2   3   4   5

           Mentally   1   2   3   4   5   About my sleep   1   2   3   4   5

How hard did I work?   1   2   3   4   5   6   7   8   9   10

Notes and reflections:

TUESDAY · DATE:

Activities/Actions:

How I felt: Physically   1   2   3   4   5   About my nutrition   1   2   3   4   5

           Mentally   1   2   3   4   5   About my sleep   1   2   3   4   5

How hard did I work?   1   2   3   4   5   6   7   8   9   10

Notes and reflections:

WEDNESDAY · DATE:

Activities/Actions:

| **How I felt:** | Physically | 1 2 3 4 5 | About my nutrition | 1 2 3 4 5 |
| | Mentally | 1 2 3 4 5 | About my sleep | 1 2 3 4 5 |

How hard did I work?   1   2   3   4   5   6   7   8   9   10

Notes and reflections:

THURSDAY · DATE:

Activities/Actions:

| **How I felt:** | Physically | 1 2 3 4 5 | About my nutrition | 1 2 3 4 5 |
| | Mentally | 1 2 3 4 5 | About my sleep | 1 2 3 4 5 |

How hard did I work?   1   2   3   4   5   6   7   8   9   10

Notes and reflections:

FRIDAY · DATE:

Activities/Actions:

How I felt:	Physically	1 2 3 4 5	About my nutrition	1 2 3 4 5
	Mentally	1 2 3 4 5	About my sleep	1 2 3 4 5

How hard did I work?   1   2   3   4   5   6   7   8   9   10

Notes and reflections:

SATURDAY · DATE:

Activities/Actions:

How I felt:	Physically	1 2 3 4 5	About my nutrition	1 2 3 4 5
	Mentally	1 2 3 4 5	About my sleep	1 2 3 4 5

How hard did I work?   1   2   3   4   5   6   7   8   9   10

Notes and reflections:

SUNDAY · DATE:

Activities/Actions:

How I felt:	Physically	1 2 3 4 5	About my nutrition	1 2 3 4 5
	Mentally	1 2 3 4 5	About my sleep	1 2 3 4 5

How hard did I work?   1   2   3   4   5   6   7   8   9   10

Notes and reflections:

Highlights/accomplishments for the week:

Actions for next week:

WEEK 8

MONDAY · DATE:

Activities/Actions:

How I felt: Physically 1 2 3 4 5   About my nutrition 1 2 3 4 5

             Mentally   1 2 3 4 5   About my sleep   1 2 3 4 5

How hard did I work?   1   2   3   4   5   6   7   8   9   10

Notes and reflections:

TUESDAY · DATE:

Activities/Actions:

How I felt: Physically 1 2 3 4 5   About my nutrition 1 2 3 4 5

             Mentally   1 2 3 4 5   About my sleep   1 2 3 4 5

How hard did I work?   1   2   3   4   5   6   7   8   9   10

Notes and reflections:

WEDNESDAY · DATE:

Activities/Actions:

How I felt:	Physically	1 2 3 4 5	About my nutrition	1 2 3 4 5
	Mentally	1 2 3 4 5	About my sleep	1 2 3 4 5

How hard did I work?   1   2   3   4   5   6   7   8   9   10

Notes and reflections:

THURSDAY · DATE:

Activities/Actions:

How I felt:	Physically	1 2 3 4 5	About my nutrition	1 2 3 4 5
	Mentally	1 2 3 4 5	About my sleep	1 2 3 4 5

How hard did I work?   1   2   3   4   5   6   7   8   9   10

Notes and reflections:

FRIDAY · DATE:

Activities/Actions:

How I felt:	Physically	1 2 3 4 5	About my nutrition	1 2 3 4 5
	Mentally	1 2 3 4 5	About my sleep	1 2 3 4 5

How hard did I work? 1 2 3 4 5 6 7 8 9 10

Notes and reflections:

SATURDAY · DATE:

Activities/Actions:

How I felt:	Physically	1 2 3 4 5	About my nutrition	1 2 3 4 5
	Mentally	1 2 3 4 5	About my sleep	1 2 3 4 5

How hard did I work? 1 2 3 4 5 6 7 8 9 10

Notes and reflections:

SUNDAY · DATE:

Activities/Actions:

| **How I felt:** | Physically | 1 2 3 4 5 | About my nutrition | 1 2 3 4 5 |
| | Mentally | 1 2 3 4 5 | About my sleep | 1 2 3 4 5 |

How hard did I work? 1 2 3 4 5 6 7 8 9 10

Notes and reflections:

Highlights/accomplishments for the week:

Actions for next week:

WEEK 9

MONDAY · DATE:

Activities/Actions:

| **How I felt:** | Physically | 1 2 3 4 5 | About my nutrition | 1 2 3 4 5 |
| | Mentally | 1 2 3 4 5 | About my sleep | 1 2 3 4 5 |

How hard did I work? 1 2 3 4 5 6 7 8 9 10

Notes and reflections:

TUESDAY · DATE:

Activities/Actions:

| **How I felt:** | Physically | 1 2 3 4 5 | About my nutrition | 1 2 3 4 5 |
| | Mentally | 1 2 3 4 5 | About my sleep | 1 2 3 4 5 |

How hard did I work? 1 2 3 4 5 6 7 8 9 10

Notes and reflections:

WEDNESDAY · DATE:

Activities/Actions:

| **How I felt:** | Physically | 1 2 3 4 5 | About my nutrition | 1 2 3 4 5 |
| | Mentally | 1 2 3 4 5 | About my sleep | 1 2 3 4 5 |

How hard did I work?   1   2   3   4   5   6   7   8   9   10

Notes and reflections:

THURSDAY · DATE:

Activities/Actions:

| **How I felt:** | Physically | 1 2 3 4 5 | About my nutrition | 1 2 3 4 5 |
| | Mentally | 1 2 3 4 5 | About my sleep | 1 2 3 4 5 |

How hard did I work?   1   2   3   4   5   6   7   8   9   10

Notes and reflections:

FRIDAY · DATE:

Activities/Actions:

| **How I felt:** | Physically | 1 2 3 4 5 | About my nutrition | 1 2 3 4 5 |
| | Mentally | 1 2 3 4 5 | About my sleep | 1 2 3 4 5 |

How hard did I work?   1   2   3   4   5   6   7   8   9   10

Notes and reflections:

SATURDAY · DATE:

Activities/Actions:

| **How I felt:** | Physically | 1 2 3 4 5 | About my nutrition | 1 2 3 4 5 |
| | Mentally | 1 2 3 4 5 | About my sleep | 1 2 3 4 5 |

How hard did I work?   1   2   3   4   5   6   7   8   9   10

Notes and reflections:

SUNDAY · DATE:

Activities/Actions:

| How I felt: | Physically | 1 | 2 | 3 | 4 | 5 | | About my nutrition | 1 | 2 | 3 | 4 | 5 |
| | Mentally | 1 | 2 | 3 | 4 | 5 | | About my sleep | 1 | 2 | 3 | 4 | 5 |

How hard did I work?   1   2   3   4   5   6   7   8   9   10

Notes and reflections:

Highlights/accomplishments for the week:

Actions for next week:

WEEK 10

MONDAY · DATE:

Activities/Actions:

| **How I felt:** | Physically | 1 | 2 | 3 | 4 | 5 | | About my nutrition | 1 | 2 | 3 | 4 | 5 |
| | Mentally | 1 | 2 | 3 | 4 | 5 | | About my sleep | 1 | 2 | 3 | 4 | 5 |

How hard did I work? 1 2 3 4 5 6 7 8 9 10

Notes and reflections:

TUESDAY · DATE:

Activities/Actions:

| **How I felt:** | Physically | 1 | 2 | 3 | 4 | 5 | | About my nutrition | 1 | 2 | 3 | 4 | 5 |
| | Mentally | 1 | 2 | 3 | 4 | 5 | | About my sleep | 1 | 2 | 3 | 4 | 5 |

How hard did I work? 1 2 3 4 5 6 7 8 9 10

Notes and reflections:

WEDNESDAY · DATE:

Activities/Actions:

| **How I felt:** | Physically | 1 2 3 4 5 | About my nutrition | 1 2 3 4 5 |
| | Mentally | 1 2 3 4 5 | About my sleep | 1 2 3 4 5 |

How hard did I work? 1 2 3 4 5 6 7 8 9 10

Notes and reflections:

THURSDAY · DATE:

Activities/Actions:

| **How I felt:** | Physically | 1 2 3 4 5 | About my nutrition | 1 2 3 4 5 |
| | Mentally | 1 2 3 4 5 | About my sleep | 1 2 3 4 5 |

How hard did I work? 1 2 3 4 5 6 7 8 9 10

Notes and reflections:

FRIDAY · DATE:

Activities/Actions:

How I felt: Physically 1 2 3 4 5   About my nutrition 1 2 3 4 5

            Mentally 1 2 3 4 5   About my sleep 1 2 3 4 5

How hard did I work? 1 2 3 4 5 6 7 8 9 10

Notes and reflections:

SATURDAY · DATE:

Activities/Actions:

How I felt: Physically 1 2 3 4 5   About my nutrition 1 2 3 4 5

            Mentally 1 2 3 4 5   About my sleep 1 2 3 4 5

How hard did I work? 1 2 3 4 5 6 7 8 9 10

Notes and reflections:

SUNDAY · DATE:

Activities/Actions:

How I felt:	Physically	1 2 3 4 5	About my nutrition	1 2 3 4 5
	Mentally	1 2 3 4 5	About my sleep	1 2 3 4 5

How hard did I work?   1   2   3   4   5   6   7   8   9   10

Notes and reflections:

Highlights/accomplishments for the week:

Actions for next week:

WEEK 11

MONDAY · DATE:

Activities/Actions:

How I felt: Physically   1   2   3   4   5   About my nutrition   1   2   3   4   5

           Mentally   1   2   3   4   5   About my sleep   1   2   3   4   5

How hard did I work?   1   2   3   4   5   6   7   8   9   10

Notes and reflections:

TUESDAY · DATE:

Activities/Actions:

How I felt: Physically   1   2   3   4   5   About my nutrition   1   2   3   4   5

           Mentally   1   2   3   4   5   About my sleep   1   2   3   4   5

How hard did I work?   1   2   3   4   5   6   7   8   9   10

Notes and reflections:

WEDNESDAY · DATE:

Activities/Actions:

| **How I felt:** | Physically | 1 2 3 4 5 | About my nutrition | 1 2 3 4 5 |
| | Mentally | 1 2 3 4 5 | About my sleep | 1 2 3 4 5 |

How hard did I work? 1 2 3 4 5 6 7 8 9 10

Notes and reflections:

THURSDAY · DATE:

Activities/Actions:

| **How I felt:** | Physically | 1 2 3 4 5 | About my nutrition | 1 2 3 4 5 |
| | Mentally | 1 2 3 4 5 | About my sleep | 1 2 3 4 5 |

How hard did I work? 1 2 3 4 5 6 7 8 9 10

Notes and reflections:

FRIDAY · DATE:

Activities/Actions:

How I felt:	Physically	1 2 3 4 5	About my nutrition	1 2 3 4 5
	Mentally	1 2 3 4 5	About my sleep	1 2 3 4 5

How hard did I work? 1 2 3 4 5 6 7 8 9 10

Notes and reflections:

SATURDAY · DATE:

Activities/Actions:

How I felt:	Physically	1 2 3 4 5	About my nutrition	1 2 3 4 5
	Mentally	1 2 3 4 5	About my sleep	1 2 3 4 5

How hard did I work? 1 2 3 4 5 6 7 8 9 10

Notes and reflections:

SUNDAY · DATE:

Activities/Actions:

| **How I felt:** | Physically | 1 2 3 4 5 | About my nutrition | 1 2 3 4 5 |
| | Mentally | 1 2 3 4 5 | About my sleep | 1 2 3 4 5 |

How hard did I work?   1   2   3   4   5   6   7   8   9   10

Notes and reflections:

Highlights/accomplishments for the week:

Actions for next week:

WEEK 12

MONDAY · DATE:

Activities/Actions:

How I felt: Physically 1 2 3 4 5   About my nutrition 1 2 3 4 5

            Mentally 1 2 3 4 5   About my sleep 1 2 3 4 5

How hard did I work? 1 2 3 4 5 6 7 8 9 10

Notes and reflections:

TUESDAY · DATE:

Activities/Actions:

How I felt: Physically 1 2 3 4 5   About my nutrition 1 2 3 4 5

            Mentally 1 2 3 4 5   About my sleep 1 2 3 4 5

How hard did I work? 1 2 3 4 5 6 7 8 9 10

Notes and reflections:

WEDNESDAY · DATE:

Activities/Actions:

| **How I felt:** | Physically | 1 2 3 4 5 | About my nutrition | 1 2 3 4 5 |
| | Mentally | 1 2 3 4 5 | About my sleep | 1 2 3 4 5 |

How hard did I work?　1　2　3　4　5　6　7　8　9　10

Notes and reflections:

THURSDAY · DATE:

Activities/Actions:

| **How I felt:** | Physically | 1 2 3 4 5 | About my nutrition | 1 2 3 4 5 |
| | Mentally | 1 2 3 4 5 | About my sleep | 1 2 3 4 5 |

How hard did I work?　1　2　3　4　5　6　7　8　9　10

Notes and reflections:

FRIDAY · DATE:

Activities/Actions:

How I felt:	Physically	1 2 3 4 5	About my nutrition	1 2 3 4 5
	Mentally	1 2 3 4 5	About my sleep	1 2 3 4 5

How hard did I work?   1   2   3   4   5   6   7   8   9   10

Notes and reflections:

SATURDAY · DATE:

Activities/Actions:

How I felt:	Physically	1 2 3 4 5	About my nutrition	1 2 3 4 5
	Mentally	1 2 3 4 5	About my sleep	1 2 3 4 5

How hard did I work?   1   2   3   4   5   6   7   8   9   10

Notes and reflections:

SUNDAY · DATE:

Activities/Actions:

| **How I felt:** | Physically | 1 2 3 4 5 | About my nutrition | 1 2 3 4 5 |
| | Mentally | 1 2 3 4 5 | About my sleep | 1 2 3 4 5 |

How hard did I work?   1   2   3   4   5   6   7   8   9   10

Notes and reflections:

Highlights/accomplishments for the week:

Actions for next week:

WEEK 13

MONDAY · DATE:

Activities/Actions:

| **How I felt:** Physically | 1 2 3 4 5 | About my nutrition | 1 2 3 4 5 |
| Mentally | 1 2 3 4 5 | About my sleep | 1 2 3 4 5 |

How hard did I work? 1 2 3 4 5 6 7 8 9 10

Notes and reflections:

TUESDAY · DATE:

Activities/Actions:

| **How I felt:** Physically | 1 2 3 4 5 | About my nutrition | 1 2 3 4 5 |
| Mentally | 1 2 3 4 5 | About my sleep | 1 2 3 4 5 |

How hard did I work? 1 2 3 4 5 6 7 8 9 10

Notes and reflections:

WEDNESDAY · DATE:

Activities/Actions:

| **How I felt:** | Physically | 1 2 3 4 5 | About my nutrition | 1 2 3 4 5 |
| | Mentally | 1 2 3 4 5 | About my sleep | 1 2 3 4 5 |

How hard did I work? 1 2 3 4 5 6 7 8 9 10

Notes and reflections:

THURSDAY · DATE:

Activities/Actions:

| **How I felt:** | Physically | 1 2 3 4 5 | About my nutrition | 1 2 3 4 5 |
| | Mentally | 1 2 3 4 5 | About my sleep | 1 2 3 4 5 |

How hard did I work? 1 2 3 4 5 6 7 8 9 10

Notes and reflections:

FRIDAY · DATE:

Activities/Actions:

| **How I felt:** | Physically | 1 2 3 4 5 | About my nutrition | 1 2 3 4 5 |
| | Mentally | 1 2 3 4 5 | About my sleep | 1 2 3 4 5 |

How hard did I work? 1 2 3 4 5 6 7 8 9 10

Notes and reflections:

SATURDAY · DATE:

Activities/Actions:

| **How I felt:** | Physically | 1 2 3 4 5 | About my nutrition | 1 2 3 4 5 |
| | Mentally | 1 2 3 4 5 | About my sleep | 1 2 3 4 5 |

How hard did I work? 1 2 3 4 5 6 7 8 9 10

Notes and reflections:

SUNDAY · DATE:

Activities/Actions:

| How I felt: | Physically | 1 2 3 4 5 | About my nutrition | 1 2 3 4 5 |
| | Mentally | 1 2 3 4 5 | About my sleep | 1 2 3 4 5 |

How hard did I work?   1   2   3   4   5   6   7   8   9   10

Notes and reflections:

Highlights/accomplishments for the week:

Actions for next week:

Congratulations! You have invested a significant amount of time and energy in your training and in recording and monitoring your thoughts, feelings, activities and actions. Take some time to think about the past 13 weeks. Consider your accomplishments, the obstacles you have overcome, your goals and your personal motivation plan.

Begin by writing anything you would like in the space provided—just let your mind and your pen wander. (If you would prefer to write about a specific topic, describe what stands out for you about the past 13 weeks.)

My thoughts at the end of 13 weeks of training:

_____

_____

_____

_____

Now examine your journal entries for the past 13 weeks and answer the following questions.

1. What have been your biggest lessons over the past 13 weeks?
2. What is your vision of yourself right now?
3. Which of your actions have moved you towards your goals or helped you overcome obstacles?
4. Which of your actions have not been helpful or have discouraged you?

Celebrate your accomplishments

Accomplishments can relate to outcomes (e.g., running farther and faster) or to the training process (e.g., consistently following your program). They can also relate to other aspects of your life. Be proud of what you have done. It is much easier to remember your accomplishments when you celebrate them.

List your accomplishments in the space provided and read them over to develop a vision of yourself, your successes and your abilities.

My accomplishments:

_____

_____

_____

Analyse the obstacles you overcame

Over the past 13 weeks you have probably experienced a few challenges. It is good to explore these to gain a better understanding of yourself. Describe these obstacles, how they affected you and how you overcame them.

Obstacles to achieving my fitness goals	How these affected me	How I overcame them

Re-examine your program goals

Take a moment and refer back to your program goals and the end points you identified—the ways you would know if you achieved your goals. Answer the following questions.

1. Did you achieve your program goals?
2. Did you give yourself the best chance for success possible?
3. What factors supported your achievements?
4. What role did your personal motivation plan play?
5. What actions could you take to continue to move towards your long-term goals?

Re-evaluate your personal motivation plan

Consider your personal motivation plan and how it worked for you throughout the program. What actions could you take to improve the following parts of your plan?

Vision/Mission

Handling obstacles

Thoughts and feelings

Social support

Cues in the environment

Rewards

Maintain your pace

You have had an opportunity to work on your fitness goals for 13 weeks. Your aim now should be to maintain your pace. In order to make fitness a routine part of your life you need to be consistently active for a minimum of six months. Right now you are halfway there and a lot farther along than you were three months ago. Good work!

Now take the lessons you have learned from the past 13 weeks and apply them to a new challenge. Choose one of the following options and set some new goals for the next 13 weeks.

Option 1: Try the 13-week run walk/program again. Circumstances may have prevented you from doing the program (see Appendix A) fully. Or maybe you really enjoyed the program and would like to see if you can do it again.

Option 2: Try the 13-week run/walk maintenance program. The maintenance program (see Appendix B) picks up where you left off with the walk/run program. By continuing with three workouts a week you can maintain the level of fitness and activity that you have already achieved.

Option 3: Try another program offered in your community or join a training group. See what your local fitness centre or running store has to offer. You may be ready for a more challenging program or you may aspire to greater running pursuits.

My program goals for the next 13 weeks:

_____

_____

Now prepare yourself to start by setting your action goals for the week ahead (Week 14).

Short-term action goals:

_____

_____

WEEK 14

MONDAY · DATE:

Activities/Actions:

How I felt: Physically 1 2 3 4 5   About my nutrition 1 2 3 4 5

Mentally 1 2 3 4 5   About my sleep 1 2 3 4 5

How hard did I work? 1 2 3 4 5 6 7 8 9 10

Notes and reflections:

TUESDAY · DATE:

Activities/Actions:

How I felt: Physically 1 2 3 4 5   About my nutrition 1 2 3 4 5

Mentally 1 2 3 4 5   About my sleep 1 2 3 4 5

How hard did I work? 1 2 3 4 5 6 7 8 9 10

Notes and reflections:

WEDNESDAY · DATE:

Activities/Actions:

| **How I felt:** | Physically | 1 2 3 4 5 | About my nutrition | 1 2 3 4 5 |
| | Mentally | 1 2 3 4 5 | About my sleep | 1 2 3 4 5 |

How hard did I work?   1   2   3   4   5   6   7   8   9   10

Notes and reflections:

THURSDAY · DATE:

Activities/Actions:

| **How I felt:** | Physically | 1 2 3 4 5 | About my nutrition | 1 2 3 4 5 |
| | Mentally | 1 2 3 4 5 | About my sleep | 1 2 3 4 5 |

How hard did I work?   1   2   3   4   5   6   7   8   9   10

Notes and reflections:

FRIDAY · DATE:

Activities/Actions:

How I felt:	Physically	1 2 3 4 5	About my nutrition	1 2 3 4 5
	Mentally	1 2 3 4 5	About my sleep	1 2 3 4 5

How hard did I work?   1   2   3   4   5   6   7   8   9   10

Notes and reflections:

SATURDAY · DATE:

Activities/Actions:

How I felt:	Physically	1 2 3 4 5	About my nutrition	1 2 3 4 5
	Mentally	1 2 3 4 5	About my sleep	1 2 3 4 5

How hard did I work?   1   2   3   4   5   6   7   8   9   10

Notes and reflections:

SUNDAY · DATE:

Activities/Actions:

| **How I felt:** | Physically | 1 2 3 4 5 | About my nutrition | 1 2 3 4 5 |
| | Mentally | 1 2 3 4 5 | About my sleep | 1 2 3 4 5 |

| **How hard did I work?** | 1 2 3 4 5 6 7 8 9 10 |

Notes and reflections:

Highlights/accomplishments for the week:

Actions for next week:

WEEK 15

MONDAY · DATE:

Activities/Actions:

How I felt: Physically 1 2 3 4 5   About my nutrition 1 2 3 4 5

           Mentally 1 2 3 4 5   About my sleep   1 2 3 4 5

How hard did I work?   1   2   3   4   5   6   7   8   9   10

Notes and reflections:

TUESDAY · DATE:

Activities/Actions:

How I felt: Physically 1 2 3 4 5   About my nutrition 1 2 3 4 5

           Mentally 1 2 3 4 5   About my sleep   1 2 3 4 5

How hard did I work?   1   2   3   4   5   6   7   8   9   10

Notes and reflections:

WEDNESDAY · DATE:

Activities/Actions:

| How I felt: | Physically | 1 2 3 4 5 | About my nutrition | 1 2 3 4 5 |
| | Mentally | 1 2 3 4 5 | About my sleep | 1 2 3 4 5 |

How hard did I work? 1 2 3 4 5 6 7 8 9 10

Notes and reflections:

THURSDAY · DATE:

Activities/Actions:

| How I felt: | Physically | 1 2 3 4 5 | About my nutrition | 1 2 3 4 5 |
| | Mentally | 1 2 3 4 5 | About my sleep | 1 2 3 4 5 |

How hard did I work? 1 2 3 4 5 6 7 8 9 10

Notes and reflections:

FRIDAY · DATE:

Activities/Actions:

| **How I felt:** | Physically | 1 | 2 | 3 | 4 | 5 | | About my nutrition | 1 | 2 | 3 | 4 | 5 |
| | Mentally | 1 | 2 | 3 | 4 | 5 | | About my sleep | 1 | 2 | 3 | 4 | 5 |

How hard did I work?   1   2   3   4   5   6   7   8   9   10

Notes and reflections:

SATURDAY · DATE:

Activities/Actions:

| **How I felt:** | Physically | 1 | 2 | 3 | 4 | 5 | | About my nutrition | 1 | 2 | 3 | 4 | 5 |
| | Mentally | 1 | 2 | 3 | 4 | 5 | | About my sleep | 1 | 2 | 3 | 4 | 5 |

How hard did I work?   1   2   3   4   5   6   7   8   9   10

Notes and reflections:

SUNDAY · DATE:

Activities/Actions:

How I felt:	Physically	1 2 3 4 5	About my nutrition	1 2 3 4 5
	Mentally	1 2 3 4 5	About my sleep	1 2 3 4 5

How hard did I work?   1   2   3   4   5   6   7   8   9   10

Notes and reflections:

Highlights/accomplishments for the week:

Actions for next week:

WEEK 16

MONDAY · DATE:

Activities/Actions:

| **How I felt:** | Physically | 1 2 3 4 5 | About my nutrition | 1 2 3 4 5 |
| | Mentally | 1 2 3 4 5 | About my sleep | 1 2 3 4 5 |

How hard did I work? 1 2 3 4 5 6 7 8 9 10

Notes and reflections:

TUESDAY · DATE:

Activities/Actions:

| **How I felt:** | Physically | 1 2 3 4 5 | About my nutrition | 1 2 3 4 5 |
| | Mentally | 1 2 3 4 5 | About my sleep | 1 2 3 4 5 |

How hard did I work? 1 2 3 4 5 6 7 8 9 10

Notes and reflections:

WEDNESDAY · DATE:

Activities/Actions:

| **How I felt:** | Physically | 1 2 3 4 5 | About my nutrition | 1 2 3 4 5 |
| | Mentally | 1 2 3 4 5 | About my sleep | 1 2 3 4 5 |

How hard did I work?   1   2   3   4   5   6   7   8   9   10

Notes and reflections:

THURSDAY · DATE:

Activities/Actions:

| **How I felt:** | Physically | 1 2 3 4 5 | About my nutrition | 1 2 3 4 5 |
| | Mentally | 1 2 3 4 5 | About my sleep | 1 2 3 4 5 |

How hard did I work?   1   2   3   4   5   6   7   8   9   10

Notes and reflections:

FRIDAY · DATE:

Activities/Actions:

| **How I felt:** Physically | 1 2 3 4 5 | About my nutrition | 1 2 3 4 5 |
| Mentally | 1 2 3 4 5 | About my sleep | 1 2 3 4 5 |

How hard did I work?   1   2   3   4   5   6   7   8   9   10

Notes and reflections:

SATURDAY · DATE:

Activities/Actions:

| **How I felt:** Physically | 1 2 3 4 5 | About my nutrition | 1 2 3 4 5 |
| Mentally | 1 2 3 4 5 | About my sleep | 1 2 3 4 5 |

How hard did I work?   1   2   3   4   5   6   7   8   9   10

Notes and reflections:

SUNDAY · DATE:

Activities/Actions:

How I felt:	Physically	1 2 3 4 5	About my nutrition	1 2 3 4 5
	Mentally	1 2 3 4 5	About my sleep	1 2 3 4 5

How hard did I work?   1   2   3   4   5   6   7   8   9   10

Notes and reflections:

Highlights/accomplishments for the week:

Actions for next week:

WEEK 17

MONDAY · DATE:

Activities/Actions:

| **How I felt:** | Physically | 1 2 3 4 5 | About my nutrition | 1 2 3 4 5 |
| | Mentally | 1 2 3 4 5 | About my sleep | 1 2 3 4 5 |

How hard did I work?   1   2   3   4   5   6   7   8   9   10

Notes and reflections:

TUESDAY · DATE:

Activities/Actions:

| **How I felt:** | Physically | 1 2 3 4 5 | About my nutrition | 1 2 3 4 5 |
| | Mentally | 1 2 3 4 5 | About my sleep | 1 2 3 4 5 |

How hard did I work?   1   2   3   4   5   6   7   8   9   10

Notes and reflections:

WEDNESDAY · DATE:

Activities/Actions:

How I felt: Physically	1 2 3 4 5	About my nutrition	1 2 3 4 5
Mentally	1 2 3 4 5	About my sleep	1 2 3 4 5

How hard did I work?   1   2   3   4   5   6   7   8   9   10

Notes and reflections:

THURSDAY · DATE:

Activities/Actions:

How I felt: Physically	1 2 3 4 5	About my nutrition	1 2 3 4 5
Mentally	1 2 3 4 5	About my sleep	1 2 3 4 5

How hard did I work?   1   2   3   4   5   6   7   8   9   10

Notes and reflections:

FRIDAY · DATE:

Activities/Actions:

How I felt:	Physically	1 2 3 4 5	About my nutrition	1 2 3 4 5
	Mentally	1 2 3 4 5	About my sleep	1 2 3 4 5

How hard did I work?   1   2   3   4   5   6   7   8   9   10

Notes and reflections:

SATURDAY · DATE:

Activities/Actions:

How I felt:	Physically	1 2 3 4 5	About my nutrition	1 2 3 4 5
	Mentally	1 2 3 4 5	About my sleep	1 2 3 4 5

How hard did I work?   1   2   3   4   5   6   7   8   9   10

Notes and reflections:

SUNDAY · DATE:

Activities/Actions:

| **How I felt:** | Physically | 1 2 3 4 5 | About my nutrition | 1 2 3 4 5 |
| | Mentally | 1 2 3 4 5 | About my sleep | 1 2 3 4 5 |

How hard did I work?   1   2   3   4   5   6   7   8   9   10

Notes and reflections:

Highlights/accomplishments for the week:

Actions for next week:

WEEK 18

MONDAY · DATE:

Activities/Actions:

How I felt: Physically   1   2   3   4   5   About my nutrition   1   2   3   4   5
            Mentally   1   2   3   4   5   About my sleep   1   2   3   4   5

How hard did I work?   1   2   3   4   5   6   7   8   9   10

Notes and reflections:

TUESDAY · DATE:

Activities/Actions:

How I felt: Physically   1   2   3   4   5   About my nutrition   1   2   3   4   5
            Mentally   1   2   3   4   5   About my sleep   1   2   3   4   5

How hard did I work?   1   2   3   4   5   6   7   8   9   10

Notes and reflections:

WEDNESDAY · DATE:

Activities/Actions:

| **How I felt:** | Physically | 1 2 3 4 5 | About my nutrition | 1 2 3 4 5 |
| | Mentally | 1 2 3 4 5 | About my sleep | 1 2 3 4 5 |

How hard did I work?   1   2   3   4   5   6   7   8   9   10

Notes and reflections:

THURSDAY · DATE:

Activities/Actions:

| **How I felt:** | Physically | 1 2 3 4 5 | About my nutrition | 1 2 3 4 5 |
| | Mentally | 1 2 3 4 5 | About my sleep | 1 2 3 4 5 |

How hard did I work?   1   2   3   4   5   6   7   8   9   10

Notes and reflections:

FRIDAY · DATE:

Activities/Actions:

How I felt: Physically	1	2	3	4	5	About my nutrition	1 2 3 4 5
Mentally	1	2	3	4	5	About my sleep	1 2 3 4 5

How hard did I work? 1 2 3 4 5 6 7 8 9 10

Notes and reflections:

SATURDAY · DATE:

Activities/Actions:

How I felt: Physically	1	2	3	4	5	About my nutrition	1 2 3 4 5
Mentally	1	2	3	4	5	About my sleep	1 2 3 4 5

How hard did I work? 1 2 3 4 5 6 7 8 9 10

Notes and reflections:

SUNDAY · DATE:

Activities/Actions:

How I felt:	Physically	1 2 3 4 5	About my nutrition	1 2 3 4 5
	Mentally	1 2 3 4 5	About my sleep	1 2 3 4 5

How hard did I work?   1   2   3   4   5   6   7   8   9   10

Notes and reflections:

Highlights/accomplishments for the week:

Actions for next week:

WEEK 19

MONDAY · DATE:

Activities/Actions:

How I felt: Physically 1 2 3 4 5   About my nutrition 1 2 3 4 5

Mentally 1 2 3 4 5   About my sleep 1 2 3 4 5

How hard did I work?   1   2   3   4   5   6   7   8   9   10

Notes and reflections:

TUESDAY · DATE:

Activities/Actions:

How I felt: Physically 1 2 3 4 5   About my nutrition 1 2 3 4 5

Mentally 1 2 3 4 5   About my sleep 1 2 3 4 5

How hard did I work?   1   2   3   4   5   6   7   8   9   10

Notes and reflections:

WEDNESDAY · DATE:

Activities/Actions:

| **How I felt:** Physically | 1 2 3 4 5 | About my nutrition | 1 2 3 4 5 |
| Mentally | 1 2 3 4 5 | About my sleep | 1 2 3 4 5 |

How hard did I work? 1 2 3 4 5 6 7 8 9 10

Notes and reflections:

THURSDAY · DATE:

Activities/Actions:

| **How I felt:** Physically | 1 2 3 4 5 | About my nutrition | 1 2 3 4 5 |
| Mentally | 1 2 3 4 5 | About my sleep | 1 2 3 4 5 |

How hard did I work? 1 2 3 4 5 6 7 8 9 10

Notes and reflections:

FRIDAY · DATE:

Activities/Actions:

How I felt: Physically 1 2 3 4 5   About my nutrition 1 2 3 4 5

Mentally 1 2 3 4 5   About my sleep 1 2 3 4 5

How hard did I work? 1 2 3 4 5 6 7 8 9 10

Notes and reflections:

SATURDAY · DATE:

Activities/Actions:

How I felt: Physically 1 2 3 4 5   About my nutrition 1 2 3 4 5

Mentally 1 2 3 4 5   About my sleep 1 2 3 4 5

How hard did I work? 1 2 3 4 5 6 7 8 9 10

Notes and reflections:

SUNDAY · DATE:

Activities/Actions:

| **How I felt:** | Physically | 1 2 3 4 5 | About my nutrition | 1 2 3 4 5 |
| | Mentally | 1 2 3 4 5 | About my sleep | 1 2 3 4 5 |

How hard did I work?   1   2   3   4   5   6   7   8   9   10

Notes and reflections:

Highlights/accomplishments for the week:

Actions for next week:

Congratulations! You have made it through another six weeks of your program. Again, it is time to think about your experience. Briefly examine your journal entries for the past six weeks

1. What were the main highlights of the past six weeks? What were your biggest accomplishments?
2. How have you been celebrating your accomplishments?
3. What were your biggest challenges of the past six weeks?
4. Which of your actions have moved you towards your goals or helped you overcome obstacles?
5. Which of your actions have not been helpful or have discouraged you?
6. Has anything happened that you did not expect?
7. What actions do you really need to focus on over the next seven weeks to help you through the process?

Now consider your personal motivation plan and how it has been working for you. What actions could you take to improve the following parts of your plan?

Vision/Mission

Handling obstacles

Thoughts and feelings

Social support

Cues in the environment

Rewards

Describe your goals for the week ahead (Week 20).

Short-term action goals:

_____

_____

_____

Take a moment to write anything you would like in this space. You can reflect further on your experience with the walk/run program or examine other aspects of your life right now.

Thoughts and reflections:

_____

_____

_____

_____

_____

_____

_____

_____

WEEK 20

MONDAY · DATE:

Activities/Actions:

How I felt: Physically 1 2 3 4 5   About my nutrition 1 2 3 4 5

Mentally 1 2 3 4 5   About my sleep 1 2 3 4 5

How hard did I work? 1 2 3 4 5 6 7 8 9 10

Notes and reflections:

TUESDAY · DATE:

Activities/Actions:

How I felt: Physically 1 2 3 4 5   About my nutrition 1 2 3 4 5

Mentally 1 2 3 4 5   About my sleep 1 2 3 4 5

How hard did I work? 1 2 3 4 5 6 7 8 9 10

Notes and reflections:

WEDNESDAY · DATE:

Activities/Actions:

| **How I felt:** | Physically | 1 2 3 4 5 | About my nutrition | 1 2 3 4 5 |
| | Mentally | 1 2 3 4 5 | About my sleep | 1 2 3 4 5 |

How hard did I work? 1 2 3 4 5 6 7 8 9 10

Notes and reflections:

THURSDAY · DATE:

Activities/Actions:

| **How I felt:** | Physically | 1 2 3 4 5 | About my nutrition | 1 2 3 4 5 |
| | Mentally | 1 2 3 4 5 | About my sleep | 1 2 3 4 5 |

How hard did I work? 1 2 3 4 5 6 7 8 9 10

Notes and reflections:

FRIDAY · DATE:

Activities/Actions:

| **How I felt:** | Physically | 1 2 3 4 5 | About my nutrition | 1 2 3 4 5 |
| | Mentally | 1 2 3 4 5 | About my sleep | 1 2 3 4 5 |

How hard did I work? 1 2 3 4 5 6 7 8 9 10

Notes and reflections:

SATURDAY · DATE:

Activities/Actions:

| **How I felt:** | Physically | 1 2 3 4 5 | About my nutrition | 1 2 3 4 5 |
| | Mentally | 1 2 3 4 5 | About my sleep | 1 2 3 4 5 |

How hard did I work? 1 2 3 4 5 6 7 8 9 10

Notes and reflections:

SUNDAY · DATE:

Activities/Actions:

| **How I felt:** | Physically | 1 2 3 4 5 | About my nutrition | 1 2 3 4 5 |
| | Mentally | 1 2 3 4 5 | About my sleep | 1 2 3 4 5 |

How hard did I work?   1   2   3   4   5   6   7   8   9   10

Notes and reflections:

Highlights/accomplishments for the week:

Actions for next week:

WEEK 21

MONDAY · DATE:

Activities/Actions:

How I felt: Physically 1 2 3 4 5   About my nutrition 1 2 3 4 5
Mentally 1 2 3 4 5   About my sleep 1 2 3 4 5

How hard did I work? 1 2 3 4 5 6 7 8 9 10

Notes and reflections:

TUESDAY · DATE:

Activities/Actions:

How I felt: Physically 1 2 3 4 5   About my nutrition 1 2 3 4 5
Mentally 1 2 3 4 5   About my sleep 1 2 3 4 5

How hard did I work? 1 2 3 4 5 6 7 8 9 10

Notes and reflections:

WEDNESDAY · DATE:

Activities/Actions:

| **How I felt:** | Physically | 1 2 3 4 5 | About my nutrition | 1 2 3 4 5 |
| | Mentally | 1 2 3 4 5 | About my sleep | 1 2 3 4 5 |

How hard did I work?   1   2   3   4   5   6   7   8   9   10

Notes and reflections:

THURSDAY · DATE:

Activities/Actions:

| **How I felt:** | Physically | 1 2 3 4 5 | About my nutrition | 1 2 3 4 5 |
| | Mentally | 1 2 3 4 5 | About my sleep | 1 2 3 4 5 |

How hard did I work?   1   2   3   4   5   6   7   8   9   10

Notes and reflections:

FRIDAY · DATE:

Activities/Actions:

| **How I felt:** | Physically | 1 2 3 4 5 | About my nutrition | 1 2 3 4 5 |
| | Mentally | 1 2 3 4 5 | About my sleep | 1 2 3 4 5 |

How hard did I work?   1   2   3   4   5   6   7   8   9   10

Notes and reflections:

SATURDAY · DATE:

Activities/Actions:

| **How I felt:** | Physically | 1 2 3 4 5 | About my nutrition | 1 2 3 4 5 |
| | Mentally | 1 2 3 4 5 | About my sleep | 1 2 3 4 5 |

How hard did I work?   1   2   3   4   5   6   7   8   9   10

Notes and reflections:

SUNDAY · DATE:

Activities/Actions:

| **How I felt:** | Physically | 1 2 3 4 5 | About my nutrition | 1 2 3 4 5 |
| | Mentally | 1 2 3 4 5 | About my sleep | 1 2 3 4 5 |

How hard did I work? 1 2 3 4 5 6 7 8 9 10

Notes and reflections:

Highlights/accomplishments for the week:

Actions for next week:

WEEK 22

MONDAY · DATE:

Activities/Actions:

How I felt:	Physically	1 2 3 4 5	About my nutrition	1 2 3 4 5
	Mentally	1 2 3 4 5	About my sleep	1 2 3 4 5

How hard did I work? 1 2 3 4 5 6 7 8 9 10

Notes and reflections:

TUESDAY · DATE:

Activities/Actions:

How I felt:	Physically	1 2 3 4 5	About my nutrition	1 2 3 4 5
	Mentally	1 2 3 4 5	About my sleep	1 2 3 4 5

How hard did I work? 1 2 3 4 5 6 7 8 9 10

Notes and reflections:

WEDNESDAY · DATE:

Activities/Actions:

How I felt: Physically 1 2 3 4 5   About my nutrition 1 2 3 4 5

           Mentally 1 2 3 4 5   About my sleep   1 2 3 4 5

How hard did I work? 1   2   3   4   5   6   7   8   9   10

Notes and reflections:

THURSDAY · DATE:

Activities/Actions:

How I felt: Physically 1 2 3 4 5   About my nutrition 1 2 3 4 5

           Mentally 1 2 3 4 5   About my sleep   1 2 3 4 5

How hard did I work? 1   2   3   4   5   6   7   8   9   10

Notes and reflections:

FRIDAY · DATE:

Activities/Actions:

| **How I felt:** | Physically | 1 2 3 4 5 | About my nutrition | 1 2 3 4 5 |
| | Mentally | 1 2 3 4 5 | About my sleep | 1 2 3 4 5 |

How hard did I work? 1 2 3 4 5 6 7 8 9 10

Notes and reflections:

SATURDAY · DATE:

Activities/Actions:

| **How I felt:** | Physically | 1 2 3 4 5 | About my nutrition | 1 2 3 4 5 |
| | Mentally | 1 2 3 4 5 | About my sleep | 1 2 3 4 5 |

How hard did I work? 1 2 3 4 5 6 7 8 9 10

Notes and reflections:

SUNDAY · DATE:

Activities/Actions:

| **How I felt:** | Physically | 1 2 3 4 5 | About my nutrition | 1 2 3 4 5 |
| | Mentally | 1 2 3 4 5 | About my sleep | 1 2 3 4 5 |

How hard did I work?   1   2   3   4   5   6   7   8   9   10

Notes and reflections:

Highlights/accomplishments for the week:

Actions for next week:

WEEK 23

MONDAY · DATE:

Activities/Actions:

How I felt: Physically	1	2	3	4	5		About my nutrition	1	2	3	4	5
Mentally	1	2	3	4	5		About my sleep	1	2	3	4	5

How hard did I work? 1 2 3 4 5 6 7 8 9 10

Notes and reflections:

TUESDAY · DATE:

Activities/Actions:

How I felt: Physically	1	2	3	4	5		About my nutrition	1	2	3	4	5
Mentally	1	2	3	4	5		About my sleep	1	2	3	4	5

How hard did I work? 1 2 3 4 5 6 7 8 9 10

Notes and reflections:

WEDNESDAY · DATE:

Activities/Actions:

How I felt:	Physically	1	2	3	4	5		About my nutrition	1	2	3	4	5
	Mentally	1	2	3	4	5		About my sleep	1	2	3	4	5

How hard did I work?   1   2   3   4   5   6   7   8   9   10

Notes and reflections:

THURSDAY · DATE:

Activities/Actions:

How I felt:	Physically	1	2	3	4	5		About my nutrition	1	2	3	4	5
	Mentally	1	2	3	4	5		About my sleep	1	2	3	4	5

How hard did I work?   1   2   3   4   5   6   7   8   9   10

Notes and reflections:

FRIDAY · DATE:

Activities/Actions:

How I felt:	Physically	1 2 3 4 5	About my nutrition	1 2 3 4 5
	Mentally	1 2 3 4 5	About my sleep	1 2 3 4 5

How hard did I work?   1   2   3   4   5   6   7   8   9   10

Notes and reflections:

SATURDAY · DATE:

Activities/Actions:

How I felt:	Physically	1 2 3 4 5	About my nutrition	1 2 3 4 5
	Mentally	1 2 3 4 5	About my sleep	1 2 3 4 5

How hard did I work?   1   2   3   4   5   6   7   8   9   10

Notes and reflections:

SUNDAY · DATE:

Activities/Actions:

How I felt:										
Physically	1	2	3	4	5	About my nutrition	1	2	3	4	5
Mentally	1	2	3	4	5	About my sleep	1	2	3	4	5

How hard did I work?   1   2   3   4   5   6   7   8   9   10

Notes and reflections:

Highlights/accomplishments for the week:

Actions for next week:

WEEK 24

MONDAY · DATE:

Activities/Actions:

How I felt: Physically   1   2   3   4   5   About my nutrition   1   2   3   4   5

Mentally   1   2   3   4   5   About my sleep   1   2   3   4   5

How hard did I work?   1   2   3   4   5   6   7   8   9   10

Notes and reflections:

TUESDAY · DATE:

Activities/Actions:

How I felt: Physically   1   2   3   4   5   About my nutrition   1   2   3   4   5

Mentally   1   2   3   4   5   About my sleep   1   2   3   4   5

How hard did I work?   1   2   3   4   5   6   7   8   9   10

Notes and reflections:

WEDNESDAY · DATE:

Activities/Actions:

| **How I felt:** | Physically | 1 2 3 4 5 | About my nutrition | 1 2 3 4 5 |
| | Mentally | 1 2 3 4 5 | About my sleep | 1 2 3 4 5 |

How hard did I work? 1 2 3 4 5 6 7 8 9 10

Notes and reflections:

THURSDAY · DATE:

Activities/Actions:

| **How I felt:** | Physically | 1 2 3 4 5 | About my nutrition | 1 2 3 4 5 |
| | Mentally | 1 2 3 4 5 | About my sleep | 1 2 3 4 5 |

How hard did I work? 1 2 3 4 5 6 7 8 9 10

Notes and reflections:

FRIDAY · DATE:

Activities/Actions:

| **How I felt:** | Physically | 1 2 3 4 5 | About my nutrition | 1 2 3 4 5 |
| | Mentally | 1 2 3 4 5 | About my sleep | 1 2 3 4 5 |

How hard did I work? 1 2 3 4 5 6 7 8 9 10

Notes and reflections:

SATURDAY · DATE:

Activities/Actions:

| **How I felt:** | Physically | 1 2 3 4 5 | About my nutrition | 1 2 3 4 5 |
| | Mentally | 1 2 3 4 5 | About my sleep | 1 2 3 4 5 |

How hard did I work? 1 2 3 4 5 6 7 8 9 10

Notes and reflections:

SUNDAY · DATE:

Activities/Actions:

| **How I felt:** | Physically | 1 2 3 4 5 | About my nutrition | 1 2 3 4 5 |
| | Mentally | 1 2 3 4 5 | About my sleep | 1 2 3 4 5 |

How hard did I work? 1   2   3   4   5   6   7   8   9   10

Notes and reflections:

Highlights/accomplishments for the week:

Actions for next week:

WEEK 25

MONDAY · DATE:

Activities/Actions:

How I felt: Physically 1 2 3 4 5   About my nutrition 1 2 3 4 5

Mentally 1 2 3 4 5   About my sleep 1 2 3 4 5

How hard did I work?   1   2   3   4   5   6   7   8   9   10

Notes and reflections:

TUESDAY · DATE:

Activities/Actions:

How I felt: Physically 1 2 3 4 5   About my nutrition 1 2 3 4 5

Mentally 1 2 3 4 5   About my sleep 1 2 3 4 5

How hard did I work?   1   2   3   4   5   6   7   8   9   10

Notes and reflections:

WEDNESDAY · DATE:

Activities/Actions:

| How I felt: | Physically | 1 2 3 4 5 | About my nutrition | 1 2 3 4 5 |
| | Mentally | 1 2 3 4 5 | About my sleep | 1 2 3 4 5 |

How hard did I work?   1   2   3   4   5   6   7   8   9   10

Notes and reflections:

THURSDAY · DATE:

Activities/Actions:

| How I felt: | Physically | 1 2 3 4 5 | About my nutrition | 1 2 3 4 5 |
| | Mentally | 1 2 3 4 5 | About my sleep | 1 2 3 4 5 |

How hard did I work?   1   2   3   4   5   6   7   8   9   10

Notes and reflections:

FRIDAY · DATE:

Activities/Actions:

How I felt:	Physically	1 2 3 4 5	About my nutrition	1 2 3 4 5
	Mentally	1 2 3 4 5	About my sleep	1 2 3 4 5

How hard did I work? 1 2 3 4 5 6 7 8 9 10

Notes and reflections:

SATURDAY · DATE:

Activities/Actions:

How I felt:	Physically	1 2 3 4 5	About my nutrition	1 2 3 4 5
	Mentally	1 2 3 4 5	About my sleep	1 2 3 4 5

How hard did I work? 1 2 3 4 5 6 7 8 9 10

Notes and reflections:

SUNDAY · DATE:

Activities/Actions:

| **How I felt:** | Physically | 1 2 3 4 5 | About my nutrition | 1 2 3 4 5 |
| | Mentally | 1 2 3 4 5 | About my sleep | 1 2 3 4 5 |

How hard did I work?   1   2   3   4   5   6   7   8   9   10

Notes and reflections:

Highlights/accomplishments for the week:

Actions for next week:

WEEK 26

MONDAY · DATE:

Activities/Actions:

How I felt: Physically 1 2 3 4 5   About my nutrition 1 2 3 4 5
           Mentally 1 2 3 4 5   About my sleep 1 2 3 4 5

How hard did I work?   1   2   3   4   5   6   7   8   9   10

Notes and reflections:

TUESDAY · DATE:

Activities/Actions:

How I felt: Physically 1 2 3 4 5   About my nutrition 1 2 3 4 5
           Mentally 1 2 3 4 5   About my sleep 1 2 3 4 5

How hard did I work?   1   2   3   4   5   6   7   8   9   10

Notes and reflections:

WEDNESDAY · DATE:

Activities/Actions:

How I felt:	Physically	1 2 3 4 5	About my nutrition	1 2 3 4 5
	Mentally	1 2 3 4 5	About my sleep	1 2 3 4 5

How hard did I work?   1   2   3   4   5   6   7   8   9   10

Notes and reflections:

THURSDAY · DATE:

Activities/Actions:

How I felt:	Physically	1 2 3 4 5	About my nutrition	1 2 3 4 5
	Mentally	1 2 3 4 5	About my sleep	1 2 3 4 5

How hard did I work?   1   2   3   4   5   6   7   8   9   10

Notes and reflections:

FRIDAY · DATE:

Activities/Actions:

How I felt: Physically 1 2 3 4 5   About my nutrition 1 2 3 4 5
            Mentally 1 2 3 4 5   About my sleep 1 2 3 4 5

How hard did I work?   1   2   3   4   5   6   7   8   9   10

Notes and reflections:

SATURDAY · DATE:

Activities/Actions:

How I felt: Physically 1 2 3 4 5   About my nutrition 1 2 3 4 5
            Mentally 1 2 3 4 5   About my sleep 1 2 3 4 5

How hard did I work?   1   2   3   4   5   6   7   8   9   10

Notes and reflections:

SUNDAY · DATE:

Activities/Actions:

| **How I felt:** | Physically | 1 2 3 4 5 | About my nutrition | 1 2 3 4 5 |
| | Mentally | 1 2 3 4 5 | About my sleep | 1 2 3 4 5 |

How hard did I work?   1   2   3   4   5   6   7   8   9   10

Notes and reflections:

Highlights/accomplishments for the week:

Actions for next week:

WEEK 26 REVIEW

Congratulations! You have successfully been active for the past six months and you have recorded and monitored your thoughts, feelings, activities and actions. Take some time to think about the past 26 weeks. Consider your goals and the lessons you learned.

Begin by writing anything you would like in the space provided—just let your mind and your pen wander. (If you would prefer to write about a specific topic, describe what stands out for you about the past 26 weeks.)

My thoughts at the end of 26 weeks of training:

_____

_____

_____

_____

_____

_____

_____

_____

_____

Now take some time to review your entire journal. Look at the entries that describe days when everything was going really well. Compare these with days when you struggled. Review those days or weeks when you did not stick to your training routine or did not record anything in your journal. All these points provide you with valuable lessons about yourself and your training. Use the thoughts recorded in your journal to help answer the following questions.

1. What did you learn about yourself over the past weeks?
2. What did you learn about your motivation over the past weeks?
3. What were the main highlights? What were your biggest accomplishments?
4. What were the factors that contributed to your highlights and accomplishments?
5. What were your biggest setbacks?
6. What were the factors that contributed to your setbacks? How did you try to overcome them?
7. What things about yourself do you feel improved over the past weeks?
8. What things about yourself do you think you still need to work on?
9. What is your vision of yourself now?

Finally, re-examine the program goals you set for yourself 26 weeks ago.

1. Did you achieve your program goals?
2. Did you give yourself the best possible chance to achieve your goals?
3. What factors supported your achievements?
4. What role did your personal motivation plan play?
5. What actions could you take to continue to move towards your fitness vision?

Maintain your gains

Don't stop now. Because you have followed a fitness regimen for the past six months, you can be confident that activity is now a regular part of your life. Take a moment to celebrate your success and then decide how you are going to continue to put your lessons into action. The best way to do this is to set some new goals and continue on down the road. Here are some suggestions for keeping yourself focused on fitness.

Choose a new target. Training for races and events is a great way to stay focused on your walking/running goals. Check out upcoming events at your local fitness centre or running store and see which ones might be fun to enter.

Try something different. When it comes to physical activity, variety is the spice of life. Learn to roller-blade, take ski or snowshoe lessons, or train for a mini triathlon. The possibilities are endless and so is your fitness potential.

Work out regularly with others. Working out with people provides motivation and enjoyment. Other walkers and runners can offer support and challenge you to improve.

Keep recording your experiences. Learning is ongoing in the same way that your development as a fit and healthy person is ongoing. Continue to record and monitor your thoughts, feelings, images and actions to maximize your learning.

Continue to dream. Perhaps you have always wanted to run a marathon or compete in a triathlon. Over the past 26 weeks you have proved to yourself that you can develop a plan, set goals, achieve those goals and learn from your experiences. Those skills are the same ones required to achieve greatness in any performance area. Keep working at your training and keep writing about your experiences. Set your sights high, have a vision and enjoy the road ahead.

THE 13-WEEK WALK/RUN PROGRAM

Welcome to the 13-week walk/run program. This carefully tested exercise plan involves three training sessions each week. You should schedule these training sessions, ranging in length from 35 to 66 minutes, throughout the week so that you have at least one day between sessions.

You will notice that the program starts gradually with lots of walking. A sports watch can help you time the walk/run segments of your sessions. If you find the pace too slow, bear with it and don't be tempted to skip ahead. You won't increase your fitness—just your risk of injury.

Please note that the times shown do not include your warm-up and cool-down, so be sure to allow extra time in your schedule for these essential components of your training.

For more detailed information on training, see the companion book to this journal, *The Beginning Runner's Handbook.* There you will find advice from coaches, nutritionists and sport medicine practitioners; tips on running hills and dressing for hot or cold weather; exercises to build your strength and flexibility; and stories about people who have made the walk/run program part of their lives.

Week 1

Session 1 (35 minutes)	Run 30 seconds. Walk 4 minutes and 30 seconds. Do this 7 times.
Session 2 (40 minutes)	Run 30 seconds. Walk 4 minutes and 30 seconds. Do this 8 times.
Session 3 (40 minutes)	Run 30 seconds. Walk 4 minutes and 30 seconds. Do this 8 times.

Week 2

Session 1 (45 minutes)	Run 1 minute. Walk 4 minutes. Do this 9 times.
Session 2 (40 minutes)	Run 1 minute. Walk 4 minutes. Do this 8 times.
Session 3 (40 minutes)	Run 1 minute. Walk 4 minutes. Do this 8 times.

Week 3

Session 1 (50 minutes)	Run 1 minute and 30 seconds. Walk 3 minutes and 30 seconds. Do this 10 times.
Session 2 (40 minutes)	Run 1 minute and 30 seconds. Walk 3 minutes and 30 seconds. Do this 8 times.
Session 3 (50 minutes)	Run 1 minute and 30 seconds. Walk 3 minutes and 30 seconds. Do this 10 times.

Week 4

Session 1 (55 minutes)	Run 2 minutes. Walk 3 minutes. Do this 11 times.
Session 2 (45 minutes)	Run 2 minutes. Walk 3 minutes. Do this 9 times.
Session 3 (50 minutes)	Run 2 minutes. Walk 3 minutes. Do this 10 times.

Week 5

Session 1 (60 minutes)	Run 2 minutes and 30 seconds. Walk 2 minutes and 30 seconds. Do this 12 times.
Session 2 (50 minutes)	Run 2 minutes and 30 seconds. Walk 2 minutes and 30 seconds. Do this 10 times.
Session 3 (50 minutes)	Run 2 minutes and 30 seconds. Walk 2 minutes and 30 seconds. Do this 10 times.

Week 6

Session 1 (65 minutes)	Run 3 minutes. Walk 2 minutes. Do this 13 times.
Session 2 (50 minutes)	Run 3 minutes. Walk 2 minutes. Do this 10 times.
Session 3 (55 minutes)	Run 3 minutes. Walk 2 minutes. Do this 11 times.

Week 7

Session 1 (60 minutes)	Run 4 minutes. Walk 2 minutes. Do this 10 times.
Session 2 (54 minutes)	Run 4 minutes. Walk 2 minutes. Do this 9 times.
Session 3 (54 minutes)	Run 4 minutes. Walk 2 minutes. Do this 9 times.

Week 8

Session 1 (60 minutes)	Run 5 minutes. Walk 1 minute. Do this 10 times.
Session 2 (48 minutes)	Run 5 minutes. Walk 1 minute. Do this 8 times.
Session 3 (54 minutes)	Run 5 minutes. Walk 1 minute. Do this 9 times.

Week 9

Session 1 (63 minutes)	Run 7 minutes. Walk 2 minutes. Do this 7 times.
Session 2 (54 minutes)	Run 7 minutes. Walk 2 minutes. Do this 6 times.
Session 3 (50 minutes)	Run 7 minutes. Walk 2 minutes. Do this 5 times.

Week 10

Session 1 (44 minutes)	Run 10 minutes. Walk 1 minute. Do this 4 times.
Session 2 (41 minutes)	Run 20 minutes. Walk 1 minute. Run 20 minutes.
Session 3 (45 minutes)	Run 22 minutes. Walk 1 minute. Run 22 minutes.

Week 11

Session 1 (51 minutes)	Run 25 minutes. Walk 1 minute. Run 25 minutes.
Session 2 (56 minutes)	Run 30 minutes. Walk 1 minute. Run 25 minutes.
Session 3 (51 minutes)	Run 40 minutes. Walk 1 minute. Run 10 minutes.

Week 12

Session 1 (66 minutes)	Run 45 minutes. Walk 1 minute. Run 20 minutes.
Session 2 (66 minutes)	Run 50 minutes. Walk 1 minute. Run 15 minutes.
Session 3 (45 minutes)	Run 45 minutes.

Week 13

Session 1 (50 minutes)	Run 50 minutes.
Session 2 (40 minutes)	Run 40 minutes.
Session 3 (60 minutes)	Complete your first 10-k event (if this is your goal) or run 60 minutes.

THE 13-WEEK WALK/RUN MAINTENANCE PROGRAM

This program is designed for people who have completed the 13-week walk/run program and want to maintain their fitness gains by staying active. You may choose to follow this program, a modified version of this program or another program altogether. Whatever you choose, remember that if you have a specific training program to follow you will be more likely to maintain your activity level.

As with the previous program, you will have three training sessions each week and you should schedule these throughout the week so that you have at least one day between sessions. Most training sessions will take about an hour to complete.

Please note that the times shown do not include your warm-up and cool-down, so be sure to allow extra time in your schedule for these essential components of your training.

For more detailed information on training, see the companion book to this journal, *The Beginning Runner's Handbook.* There you will find advice from coaches, nutritionists and sport medicine practitioners; tips on running hills and dressing for hot or cold weather; exercises to build your strength and flexibility; and stories about people who have made the walk/run program part of their lives.

Week 1

Session 1 (42 minutes)	Run 4 minutes. Walk 2 minutes. Do this 7 times.
Session 2 (48 minutes)	Run 4 minutes. Walk 2 minutes. Do this 8 times.
Session 3 (48 minutes)	Run 4 minutes. Walk 2 minutes. Do this 8 times.

Week 2

Session 1 (42 minutes)	Run 5 minutes. Walk 1 minute. Do this 7 times.
Session 2 (48 minutes)	Run 5minutes. Walk 1 minute. Do this 8 times.
Session 3 (54 minutes)	Run 5minutes. Walk 1 minute. Do this 9 times.

Week 3

Session 1 (45 minutes)	Run 7 minutes. Walk 2 minutes. Do this 5 times.
Session 2 (45 minutes)	Run 7 minutes. Walk 2 minutes. Do this 5 times.
Session 3 (54 minutes)	Run 7 minutes. Walk 2 minutes. Do this 6 times.

Week 4

Session 1 (44 minutes)	Run 10 minutes. Walk 1 minute. Do this 4 times.
Session 2 (52 minutes)	Run 12 minutes. Walk 1 minute. Do this 4 times.
Session 3 (44 minutes)	Run 10 minutes. Walk 1 minute. Do this 4 times.

Week 5

Session 1 (48 minutes)	Run 15 minutes. Walk 1 minute. Do this 3 times.
Session 2 (51 minutes)	Run 16 minutes. Walk 1 minute. Do this 3 times.
Session 3 (54 minutes)	Run 17 minutes. Walk 1 minute. Do this 3 times.

Week 6

Session 1 (41 minutes)	Run 20 minutes. Walk 1 minute. Run 20 minutes.
Session 2 (43 minutes)	Run 22 minutes. Walk 1 minute. Run 20 minutes.
Session 3 (43 minutes)	Run 22 minutes. Walk 1 minute. Run 20 minutes.

Week 7

Session 1 (30 minutes)	Run 30 minutes.
Session 2 (30 minutes)	Run 30 minutes.
Session 3 (35 minutes)	Run 35 minutes.

Week 8

Session 1 (33 minutes)	Run 35 minutes.
Session 2 (30 minutes)	Run 30 minutes.
Session 3 (35 minutes)	Run 35 minutes.

Week 9

Session 1 (41 minutes)	Run 30 minutes. Walk 1 minute. Run 10 minutes.
Session 2 (46 minutes)	Run 30 minutes. Walk 1 minute. Run 15 minutes.
Session 3 (46 minutes)	Run 30 minutes. Walk 1 minute. Run 15 minutes.

Week 10

Session 1 (46 minutes)	Run 35 minutes. Walk 1 minute. Run 10 minutes.
Session 2 (51 minutes)	Run 30 minutes. Walk 1 minute. Run 20 minutes.
Session 3 (51 minutes)	Run 30 minutes. Walk 1 minute. Run 20 minutes.

Week 11

Session 1 (40 minutes)	Run 40 minutes.
Session 2 (45 minutes)	Run 45 minutes.
Session 3 (40 minutes)	Run 40 minutes.

Week 12

Session 1 (56 minutes)	Run 45 minutes. Walk 1 minute. Run 10 minutes.
Session 2 (61 minutes)	Run 45 minutes. Walk 1 minute. Run 15 minutes.
Session 3 (61 minutes)	Run 45 minutes. Walk 1 minute. Run 15 minutes.

Week 13

Session 1 (35 minutes)	Run 35 minutes.
Session 2 (40 minutes)	Run 40 minutes.
Session 3 (60 minutes)	Complete a 10-k event (if this is your goal) or run 60 minutes.